Half the Path

Minehead to Penzance in 9 days.
Via the pub.

Richard Meston

First paperback edition November 2021

(Amazon) ISBN: 979-8-7506-4422-3

Independently published

For Mum. She did like a good English essay.

Table of Contents

Acknowledgements

This book would not be possible without a serious amount of tolerance of my daftness by my family. They've had to put up with me banging on about training, tents, shoes and bags, and then breathed a sigh of relief when I finally left for 3 weeks only to return early. What's more, they've tolerated – so far without any sort of violence – my occasional mention of "I'm writing a book". To you all, I am very grateful.

I also need to thank members of the South West Coast Path Facebook group for being such a decent bunch of people and really helping. It's rare to have a Facebook group that doesn't descend into moaning and bitching, but despite being very active, every member is really supportive. Definitely a great resource if you're looking to tackle part – or all - of "The Path".

Special mention goes to Dani Blackie (current solo female record holder) and Lee Rulton (completed the path in 20 days raising over £15,000 for charity) for taking the time to chat and for their invaluable advice, and also Paul Allen for his superb videos of his walks on the SWCP which really helped jog my memory about certain sections.

A huge thank you to Chris Snell for joining me on the path for a good few days. I truly enjoyed your company, appreciated your help and it was fantastic to catch up again after so many years.

And to Howard Lucas, for the few hours from Newquay to Perranporth, thanks also! We talked about so many topics in a short time, and I still need to look up those books and podcasts you mentioned

And I suppose I ought to thank the people I occasionally try to keep up with while running. Mark for the most offensive sort of encouragement possible, and Pat for advice and inspiration. And both of you, for taking the piss before, during and after my little adventure - it all helps (apparently).

And finally to my wife, Eva, and Andy Pridmore for taking the time to read through drafts of this book and give great feedback – very much appreciated!

Prologue

I finally got to the end of the American Road, my feet thankful not to be walking on broken bricks, potholes and gravel any more. The light was almost gone, and it was dawning on me that I'd walked past the best areas to camp a few miles back. But one simply does *not go back*.

I rounded a corner into a car park and finally, there at the back was a perfect spot to camp, hidden in the bushes away from prying eyes! There was just one problem… judging by the tissues and foil wrappers all over the floor, it looked like this was the perfect spot for more than just camping and I was quite frankly too damn tired for that sort of nonsense.

With 36 miles walked so far, I needed to get my head down and recover ready for another 35 miles tomorrow. The campsites, B&B's and hotels in town were full, and what lay in front of me was a narrow road with marsh on one side and a lagoon on the other. With a wave of physical and mental exhaustion, the situation overwhelmed me and I began to panic. How the hell was I going to keep going like this for another 19 days?

Introduction

This was never supposed to be a book.

In September 2021, I went for a bit of a wander on Britain's longest national trail - the South West Coast Path. I made a few notes so I wouldn't forget everything, then when I got back, I started writing some words with the intention of turning it into a short blog post about my adventure.

After banging the keyboard for a bit longer than I intended, I checked the word count out of curiosity - 21,000 words. What started as a blog post turned into a kind of therapy, a way for me to relive the highs and lows of my adventure, and a few days later I was past forty thousand words and thinking things were getting a bit out of hand.

And here I sit with over two hundred pages of slightly more refined waffle in front of me. It's gone from "I did this, I did that" to hopefully something that vaguely conveys what it's like to walk a chunk of the wonderful, brutal, beautiful, hilly, sandy, wet, rough and comforting coast path.

There's a huge amount of interesting history along the path too; I've tried to add some of this into my story.

1

I've never written a book before, so I hope you like it. I've kept it as true as my memory can recall, with maybe one or two minor embellishments for comedy or dramatic effect. Although, to be honest, my navigation skills should provide more than enough comedy content for a few books.

There's a website which goes alongside this book at

swcpplod.co.uk

It's got some older blog posts (which are mentioned in this book), as well as all the photos I took along the way, organised by day. Most of the photos have map links which you can click to see exactly where they were taken. It's worth popping over occasionally – I make quite a few references to photos I took, and on the website you can see what I was waffling on about for yourself.

There's also a contact form on the site if you want to give any feedback, it would be great to hear from you!

CHAPTER 1
T minus 6 months

I've had a stupid idea. I'm known for them. But this one is quite the stupidest of them all.

Does anyone fancy a walk? Just something quick and easy, say... 630-ish miles along rough coastal terrain, climbing 4 times the height of Everest in an area known for some fairly changeable weather. Yes? Oh good!

I live in Dorset, fairly near to South Haven Point which is one end of the 630-mile South West Coast Path. I've had a lot of dealings with the path in my life, from walks in Swanage and Durlston as a child to trail runs around the spectacular and hilly Lulworth Ranges. I've even been at Land's End during ultra-running races in the middle of freezing January nights on more than one occasion. It gets under your skin a bit. But I'd never really thought that walking or running the whole path in one go was a terribly sensible idea.

Then with the Covid pandemic, all the running events I'd entered had been cancelled, and then cancelled again, and I was getting to the point where I was trying to find some kind of adventure, one I could do that wasn't under someone else's control and wasn't likely to be pulled away at the last moment. I joined the South West Coast Path Facebook group more with the intention of researching and finding one or two different smaller sections I could run on, but when I was faced with so many people walking great sections of the path - or even the whole lot - my brain started twitching with the idea and things snowballed from there.

Back in March of 2021, the idea was forming but the details were cloudy. I started a blog with the intention of writing down some thoughts including some of the process of going from the original idea to actually getting out the door and doing it. There were a lot of questions to answer, so I wrote down my thoughts in a blog post:

Blog Post, 19th March 2021:

Which Direction?

The path runs from Minehead in Somerset to Poole in Dorset, passing through North Devon, Cornwall, South Devon then back into Dorset.

While the start is generally considered to be Minehead and most books and websites you find give details in this direction, there is always the option of starting at Poole. I think, however, I've got a strong pull to ending at Poole as it's very close to where I live. Logistically, this simplifies the end by meaning someone could meet me and I only have half an hour to be back at home.

All in one go or split it up?

My cousin Culvin ran the path a couple of years ago, taking 22 days in total, spread over about 4 months. I'll be using his Strava traces for some planning later, but from memory he did a few 6-day stints, some weekends and a few chunks of 3 or 4 days where they fitted.

I'm lucky enough to work for myself, and I usually like getting on with something once I start it, so my intention at the moment is to do the whole thing in one go.

Initially I thought about 21 days as it's a nice round number that's not too unrealistic, but then I've got a bit nervous looking at some people far better at running than me not managing that amount of mileage, so started contemplating 25 days.

But I'm also starting to think that if I make the days longer, keep my itinerary flexible (more on that below), and intend to fast-walk most of it, running where it's more comfortable, then I should really be able to managed it in a fairly fast time.

Camp or B&B?

This one is a bit awkward.

On the one hand, B&B every night would be bloody expensive. And it defines a strict itinerary. And if my leg falls off on day 3 then that's a lot of money down the drain as I doubt B&B's will give short notice refunds.

So camping sounds like a great idea. Except for a few things. First, I hate camping. But I could get over that if it had enough benefit. Second, if I camp, I have to carry gear – tent, sleeping bag etc. Now that doesn't have to be heavy if you're willing to sacrifice comfort – I have a kit list from someone who did the SWCP in 26 days and their bag weight was 5kg including everything they needed for the whole trip (bar food and water obviously).

And camping gives you – in theory – much more flexibility. I've never done it, but apparently you can get away with pitching quietly after dark and leaving before sunrise in secluded places. That means you can see how you feel in a day, and if things are going well and I fancy another hour or two walking, that could be another few miles under the belt before bedding down for the night compared to being artificially constrained by a timetable that I made up too early.

And right now, I'm swaying towards camping. The idea of being totally self-sufficient really appeals… Now… As I'm sitting in a warm room, on a comfy chair, typing this. I'm sure on the 17th night of doing it won't carry quite as much charm…

Logistically, too, I'd need a plug for a few hours at least every 4 or 5 days in order to charge my battery pack so I can keep GPS, phone, MP3 player etc alive.

So my thoughts at the moment are to look at places to camp for about 4 days in a row, then a B&B. But again, keep an open mind.

As time went on, I ended up with maps, spreadsheets and notes everywhere. I researched each bit of kit, starting with a list of potentials then reading reviews and watching YouTube videos to narrow things down. But you can never quite tell whether something will be right for *you* until you actually try it out so I had to take a punt on various items to see how I got on with them.

I started off with the most important thing to a techy gadget-obsessed lunatic like me: a GPS with a big screen, two-way satellite communications and a big orange SOS button I could push when I fell off a cliff into the sea.

I'm not an experienced tentist, so to start getting more used to it I borrowed a small tent from my sister as well as a lightweight sleeping bag, and I bought a cheap light inflatable mattress.

From running races I've done in the past I've got various vest-style packs up to 12 litre capacity. That's fine for a day or so where you get food and water enroute and don't need to carry a tent, sleeping bag and air mat, but I was going to need something a lot bigger than that for a multi-*week* self-supported adventure. Over time, my plan became set on being a "walk with some running", rather than the focus being on running the route. But coming from a background of running and wanting to have the option to run for at least some of it, I looked at "fast-packing" packs which are designed for longer multi-day adventures but still allow you to run. At around £150 for these packs, it's not an easy decision and I had a tendency to get into a bit of analysis-paralysis

- if I chose the wrong one, I'd have to spend *another* £150 to try the next one... but how could I decide which one was right without trying it out? I had to pick one and opted for the *Ultimate Direction Fastpack 30* pack which had good reviews and the (familiar to runners) ability to stick a couple of water bottles at the front of the pack for easy access.

By researching what other people were carrying on longer hikes, I came up with a target pack weight of around 10kg. This was heavier than the "ultralight" tribe, with their crisp-packet tents and featherweight mats, but not as much as some people who seemed to be carrying the best part of 20kg and wondered why it was hard work! I had run with up to 6kg on my back, but with training I reckoned I would be able to sustain lugging 10kg on my back for long days over a few weeks.

In the end, I didn't actually try out the tent I borrowed from my sister as I quickly realised that at 2.5kg it would end up constituting more than a quarter of the pack contents weight. I'd found a few alternatives and bought the *Alpkit Soloist* tent which weighed in at around 1.2kg and I could split into its component parts of poles, flysheet and inner to spread nicely around my pack between other items.

By this time, I had firmed up the plan to be the full path from Minehead to Poole over 21 days. Now I had a fixed length, I picked a slot on the calendar between the kids going back to school (when I thought the path might be quieter), and finishing before my daughter's birthday in late September. I figured the weather would be moderate then as well, not too cold but potentially a bit wet. And from researching the facilities enroute, it looked like a lot of shops, cafes and ferries were all still open through September.

Over the next few months, I tried out and refined kit choices. I camped in the garden on several occasions. The first one in the Soloist tent with the borrowed sleeping bag was a bit of a wake-up call. The temperature that night at the end of April dropped to -2°C, and I lay awake at 4am curled into a ball trying to blow on myself to warm up, but there was no heat in my breath. At that point I decided I should probably invest in a warmer sleeping bag! I spent a long time looking for a new one, constantly being put off by the cost - in the end Eva, my wife and the only one of us with common-sense - pointed out that it was a critical bit of kit that could make or break the whole adventure, so she found one of the warmth and weight I'd been looking for and I duly dropped about £300 on a fancy bag of feathers.

The nights in the tent also gave me an opportunity to figure out the inflatable sleeping mat I had was not really right for me. It was lightweight with a dimpled surface, which is fine if you sleep on your back. But I tend to move around when sleeping, and when I ended up lying on my side, my hips and shoulders were in contact with the ground through the flatter sections of the mat and it got uncomfortable in the night. I bought a different cheap mat which was a little thicker and a tiny bit heavier, but had long baffles running from head to foot so there was no chance of touching the ground. There was a problem, though. I don't know what material it was made of but it was *incredibly* slippery. Everywhere in my garden is on at least a slight slant, and although I really tried to stick with the new mat (no pun intended!), I was constantly ending up against the tent wall as the mat and sleeping bag slowly slid to the lowest point.

The tent itself was a good shape and size for me, but there wasn't much of a porch so stowing my bag and shoes for the night became a bit of an issue - basically, my pack would have to end up in the main section with me. I was also a bit worried about the poles. They were a one-piece arrangement with about 15 individual sections of metal tubes and joints held together with elasticated rope that popped into a sort-of H shape. On the one hand, it was very quick to pop up and then bend the four corners into the holes in the tent footprint, making up an inner tent frame in literally seconds without needing any pegs. You could then hang the outer of the tent over and, if necessary, be out of the rain within about 2 minutes of taking the tent out of the pack. But my concern was that if the poles broke in any way - if they bent, or the inner rope snapped - I'd be left with no way to put the tent up at all. One special custom set of poles, lots of stressed connections, potentially more than 20 nights of setting up and taking down… I didn't like the odds of not having a single issue all the way to the end and I liked even less the idea of trying to fashion some kind of repair in the lashing rain and howling wind.

At one point I was toying with the idea of a bivvy bag. The stealth aspect of a bag sounded awesome and lent itself well to my nervous nature with regards to getting "caught" wild camping. Armed with a bivvy bag, tarp, super-slippery inflatable mattress and my sleeping bag I headed off to Dartmoor for a test night with my two boys (who were 12 and 17 at the time) and had an absolutely brilliant time. I also learnt a few things, like to check that the ground you're on is flat, and if you *have* to set up on a slope, then *definitely* have your head at the top. Trying to sleep in a bivvy bag, on a slope, head down, with a Teflon-like sleeping mattress means you spend all night sliding out of the bag and not getting much sleep! But above was a moonless night, so far away from towns that the millions of stars of the Milky Way were clear to the naked eye so I didn't really care that I was getting no sleep - I was mesmerised by the sky!

A bit more research on bivvies suggested that they are prone to condensation as they only have a single skin, and while it wasn't a problem for that single dry night on Dartmoor, I did have serious doubts over the idea of bivvying for 21 nights.

Some tents I'd looked at used a walking pole to support, but most were quite a few hundred pounds to buy. One particular Chinese option - the *Lanshan 1* - kept getting mentioned on various camping Facebook groups I was a member of and, after watching some YouTube videos, I liked the look of it so much I opted to buy one. It used a single walking pole for support in the middle of the tent, so all you had to carry was just the inner and outer fabric which packed down small and weighed in at around 800g. Better still, if you buy one direct from China it costs less than £100, but also takes something like 6 weeks to get over to the UK. I didn't have enough time to wait and then still be able to give the tent a good test, so I picked one up from Amazon with next-day delivery for about £50 more.

Physically, I'm reasonably fit. I've been running for about the last 25 years, a bit more seriously for the last 15. I started taking a fancy to ultra-distance events (those over 26.2 miles) in 2014, and have since completed several 100 mile runs, my crowning glory being a 6th place finish in the 145-mile *Kennet and Avon Canal Race* in 2019.

For the last several years I've been averaging around 40 to 50 miles per week, so I have a decent base of fitness. Because I'm not a front-of-the-pack competitor, I'd made a point of walking during my training for long events to improve efficiency and speed as I knew it would be a key component of any long race I did. In April, I decided on my training plan: I would increase my running miles for the next 4 weeks to a minimum of 60 miles per week, and then start shifting the focus from purely running to adding in an increasing amount of walking with a full-weight pack, building up the overall time I was training each week.

In May I ran 230 miles and walked around 40 miles, and by August I had swayed the balance to 110 miles of walking and 105 miles of running in the first 3 weeks of the month, covering 80 miles for the last week of training. As a family, we went for a week's holiday in Bude in early August which gave me an opportunity to run a few times both north to Sharpnose Point where the big GCHQ dishes dominate the horizon, and south to Widemouth Bay. For a few days before I left for Minehead, we also stayed in Dartmoor, and I did as little walking as I could get away with as a relaxing taper before all hell broke loose the following week!

In July, I gave all my kit and plans a test with a 30 mile walk from Swanage to Osmington to camp for a night and then walk back the next day. The walk went well. It was a very hot day with no shade from the blazing July sunshine, and I went far too fast, covering the 30 miles about 2 hours quicker than I had intended, but I got to the campsite feeling not overly tired which was important as I had the return trip to do the following day. My shoulders, however, absolutely hated me. The *Fastpack* bag had quite narrow and not very padded shoulder straps and no hip support, and when loaded with 10kg of gear and water for around 9 hours, my shoulders ended up smashed to bits.

The Lanshan tent worked very well though, and having tried it out a few times in the garden I was getting quite quick at putting it up. Again though, even on the flat ground of a campsite I was sliding around on that slippery sleeping mat during the night. As a possible solution to the problem, I'd even stuck lines of silicone sealant down to both sides of the mat to hopefully add some tackiness and keep the mat still, but within minutes they'd mostly rubbed off and just littered the floor of the tent. I made a point to research an alternative mat when I got home as this just wasn't going to work.

When I woke up in my tent the next day, I was feeling less happy. I struggled to get motivated to leave, and when I did get going, I felt like I was plodding along way too slowly with no energy, not really enjoying myself. I decided I'd learnt a lot from the first day and the night in the campsite, and didn't really need to walk all the way back to Swanage. Also, I'd suddenly remembered there was a critical requirement to watch *Avengers: Endgame* with my youngest while having a Sunday afternoon beer on the sofa (funny how I'd forgotten that one!), so called Eva for a pickup around Lulworth, having covered 12 miles instead of the planned 30.

Over the following days, my confidence took a hit because of the failure to complete the back-to-back days. I felt that if I couldn't even complete 2 days of 30 miles, why was I even *contemplating* 21 of them in a row? But to counter that argument, I had done it too fast, on a very hot day... and it occurred to me that a year or so before, I'd covered 145 miles in a race in less than 36 hours - coming 6th out of 66 starters - having not run more than about 30 miles in a single run during training... so one blip didn't necessarily mean I *couldn't* do it.

I also knew I needed a different pack. My collarbone was glowing red and swollen after the two days of walking, there was no way that was sustainable for multiple days. With all the further planning, my focus had shifted away from running and more towards walking, so instead of looking at running packs I investigated lightweight walking ones and settled on an *Osprey Talon*. Another thing I'd learnt from training was that the 30 litres of the Fastpack was not quite enough - I could just about fit everything in, but it was a tight squeeze and the zips looked like they were stretched to near breaking point. I also had no room to stick the odd pasty or other snacks that I would pick up on the way. The Talon pack was available in a few sizes, but more importantly I could actually go and see it in the shop rather than buying online - actually *try it out* and check it felt good before spending another big wodge of cash. So, a visit to Cotswold Outdoors came next and I picked up a Talon 44 litre pack which had almost 50% more capacity than the Fastpack.

The South West Coast Path Association (SWCPA) guide book - which you get for free when you join up - splits the path into 52 sections and has great information about the route in each of these areas. I started with a plan to double up the SWCPA book sections into 26 parts and then reduce those down further to figure out the end points for each of my 21 days, but it didn't really work very well like that. Even with the full A-Z book set of Ordnance Survey maps at my disposal, it was really difficult to visualise the combined distance *and* elevation, and plan days that would be achievable for three full weeks.

My day job is writing computer software, and I love analysing things, so it wasn't long before I had an idea… I created a data file containing the full route including elevation data for the whole of the South West Coast Path by joining data from various sources - runs I'd done myself, my cousin's routes and also the route taken by Kristian Morgan who is the current South West Coast Path (SWCP) record holder (completing the whole route in just 10 days 12 hours!) With the track details in the computer,

I wrote a program that would determine how far I could get in a set time, taking into account *my* actual walking pace, the slowing down from both going up and down the hills, and tiredness as the day went on. It then spat out a twenty-something page document with start and end points for each day, snippets of the OS Maps for key points, links to Google Maps so I could click and explore further, ferry timetables and even a list of campsites within 500m of the path close to the end-point each day, all automatically. I was (and still am) quite pleased with that bit of software! It gave me the opportunity to tweak things - like make every day 50 kilometres, or see how it worked out if I did 11 hours each day - then press a button and 10 seconds later I had a new document and updated set of days. After much fiddling, I finalised the plan for 11-and-a-half hours each day, with some manual adjustments around the river crossings, which I originally called *The Plan*.

The end points were picked as the result of a bunch of calculations, the computer had no idea at all whether they were in sensible places to stop or not. What I had hoped was that armed with the information in the document, I could use it as a guide to adjust for accommodation up or down the path a little, or to pick spots near for wild camping.

Although I love the analytics and data processing, I did get a bit bored with the exact details after a while, so in the end I decided I'd planned enough and I would figure out where exactly to stop each day when I actually got there and could see what my options were. Surely it would be easy to find somewhere to eat and a spot to camp on the coast path? In hindsight, this was a bit of a mistake.

Sometime in August I posted about my South West Coast Path adventure on Facebook and a few hours later I got an unexpected message from Chris, a great friend from university who I hadn't seen for 5 or 6 years. He asked if he could join me for at least some of the route. It wasn't what I'd had planned, but we spoke on the phone for a couple of hours about all sorts of things as well as actually walking the coast path. It was clear he had a lot of experience of multi-day expeditions, and he was very capable of managing himself. His concern was my planned pace - he wasn't sure he'd be able to keep going at that speed. But neither was I to be honest, and we agreed on "Top Gear Rules" - if one of us felt like going on faster, then off we went, and the other one can sort themselves out.

One thing Chris did mention during our phone call was that he had a *Nemo Tensor* sleeping mat that he was very happy with. It was one of the ones I had looked at through my research but had dismissed on price. With only a few weeks before I set off, and still needing a better inflatable mat than the one I'd been using, I looked again and found that Nemo had an option for a wide version of the Tensor mat and it was highly regarded on various forums and groups online. One of the issues with the other mats I'd tried was that they were narrow enough that my arms were constantly falling off the sides onto the cold hard ground, and the thought of a mat that was wider and I could lie on comfortably - arms and all - was quite appealing. Despite the higher price, I took the plunge and bought one.

With a couple of weeks to go, I tested my final kit choices out in the garden on 2 consecutive nights. While not a perfect night's sleep, I was happy with the decisions. The tent was working well - it was spacious, had a porch to put my bag under, only relied on 1 pole and I was getting quick at putting it up. The sleeping bag was keeping me nice and warm, and was light and packed down very small. The new Tensor air mat was made with a plastic that had enough friction to stop it slipping around in the tent, and was wide enough to be considerably more comfortable than any of the other mats I'd tried - definitely a good choice! And my pack held everything it needed with some room to spare for pastry-based snacks and, during all the training I'd done, had been pretty comfortable to wear.

I was as ready as I was going to be. I just needed to get on with it now!

CHAPTER 2
Three Trains and a Bus

Wish me luck. I've got to go 93 miles by British public transport.

Thirty years ago, I used to have drum lessons, and I got to be quite good at banging the kit. Nowadays, I tend to just tap things a lot because my drum kit has been commandeered by my son Oz who, at the age of 12, has far surpassed my ability. Very recently, he's just attained a merit at Grade 6, having played superbly along to Love Rears Its Ugly Head (Living Colour), Smells Like Teen Spirit (Nirvana) and Wake Up (Rage Against the Machine). His drum lesson is every Saturday morning, and as they're over a Zoom video-call at the moment due to this never-ending pandemic, I usually set up the computer for him. I'm not quite sure why - he's better at that than me too and it's my bloody job!

This Saturday was a bit different though. Before his lesson was due to start, I'd be getting a lift to Poole train station to begin an epic and arduous journey, hundreds of miles, hours and hours of sitting and waiting, a journey few people have written about: I was going to Minehead, by British public transport.

I was also going to wander along some path, so I might as well write something about that here too I suppose. My pack was, well… packed. My water bottles were filled, although as I write this, I'm not quite sure why - I could have made it all lighter and just filled them at Minehead. My gadgets were charged. My walking poles were ready, which again was silly as I was about to spend all day on a train and bus and I'd probably poke someone's eye out waving sticks about, so I collapsed them down and strapped them to the back of my pack. My shoes, socks, even my underpants were all at least 90% correctly applied. I WAS READY!

I said goodbye to a couple of uninterested children (they were mine, not just some random ones on the street) and got in the car with my wife Eva, who was going to eject me at the local train station.

It was finally here, the start of an adventure I'd been planning - no… *obsessing about* - for 6 months. Hours and hours of planning, more hours of boring my family and friends, and even more hours thinking about it and trying not to open my mouth for fear of tipping them over the edge with my incessant obsession. Now I was in the car, about to leave the comfort of my home for potentially 21 days of wild camping and self-sufficiency.

We got to the station, and I could see tears welling up in Eva's eyes as we said goodbye. In all my obsession with this big event

- all the planning for sleeping, eating, the training, the maps and the routes and the timings - I hadn't really stopped to think about how it might affect everyone else. It was a slam back to the huge emotions we felt those times we said goodbye for a week or two at a time when I was at university many, many years ago.

I got out of the car, got my bag from the boot and kissed Eva goodbye. Watching her drive away, the emotions and nervous butterflies in my stomach, starting me thinking about whether I was doing the right thing? It's one hell of an opportunity to be able to walk - both figuratively and very literally - away from your life for 3 weeks to scratch some ridiculous itch, a need to test yourself, a need to explore the world. But was it in any way fair to leave 4 people behind for that time, not helping out at home, not being there if they needed me?

The train was 7 minutes late. It's England - all trains are late.

The first leg was half an hour from Poole to Dorchester South and passed quickly. I sat thoughtfully looking out the window at the water, trees and houses, contemplating whether I should be doing this at all. I could just get off the train at Dorchester and go back home, and that would be that. I wouldn't be abandoning any responsibilities... and I wouldn't have to face what lay ahead.

But then I switched, I had a word with myself. There were going to be plenty of times when I'd feel down, and I needed to get over them. This whole thing wasn't going to be *any* sort of success without a serious amount of positivity, so it was time now to stop mulling over negative thoughts and instead to look forward and get excited and get going.

I caught an earlier train than I needed for my next connection so I could grab some breakfast in Dorchester. With 13kg of fresh pack on my back I wandered a mile or so up to the Wetherspoons pub, picked a seat, whipped out my phone, fired up the app and ordered a coffee and cooked breakfast. Within 90 seconds, an empty coffee cup was delivered to my table. The hot-drinks system was a fill-it-yourself-until-you-have-a-caffeine-overdose one, but the fill-it-up machine was at the far end of the bar. The bar was up some steps, round a corner and about as far away from where I was as it was possible to be and still be in the same building. Next to me on the chair, my pack had everything in it - literally *everything* I needed for the next 3 weeks. It was my house, my clothes, my food, my connection to the world, my navigation and more. It was precious. So, I went to sling it over my shoulder when the lady opposite me said "Don't worry love, I'll keep an eye on your bag."

I'm a bit awkward socially, and now I was in a socially awkward situation. If I took the pack, it meant I didn't trust her... but I didn't know her, so how could I trust her? And what did I care if she thought I didn't trust her? I'm a naturally fairly nervous person and I can see how pretty much any situation can go horribly wrong - she might grab my bag and run out the pub (after all, anyone can leg it with just 13kg right?). But my sensible brain kicked back in again: to get through this adventure I was going to have to suppress a lot of those sorts of feelings, I was going to have to do things that made me nervous. I thought there's *bound* to be times where I have to trust my fellow human beings to be nice people over the next few weeks so I might as well start now. And the pack was bloody heavy, and I'd only be a minute.

I thanked the lady, walked to the far end of the bar and filled up my cup from the slowest coffee machine in Northern Europe, and returned to not only find that no-one had stolen my bag or all its contents, but someone had left me a huge plate of fried breakfast! And very nice it was too. I wasn't all that hungry having not really done anything other than sit on a train for half an hour then walk a mile, but it went down well and along with the coffee I felt ready to tackle anything. Which was handy, because I had to tackle *Great Western Railway* running my next train.

The walk back down to Dorchester West station was through the lovely Borough Gardens which I didn't even know existed despite living only a short distance from Dorchester most of my life and having visited many times. On the walk down, my pack felt like it was settling in on my back, like it weighed a little less although it was still heavy enough for me to wonder how the hell I was going to lug this lot for over 600 miles.

Crossing the road I headed for Domino's Pizza, which is the cunning disguise for Dorchester West train station (situated just behind Domino's but not obvious until you get close). In 1989, the *Daily Telegraph* described Dorchester West as 'one of the country's worst railway stations, with graffiti everywhere and decaying walls', but now it just looks like a fairly tidy little station with 2 platforms, a bridge, a few planters and the usual array of railway-related signs. I crossed the bridge to the other side and as I stepped onto the platform, I was greeted by an announcement that my next train was 17 minutes late. All was normal in the world.

I found a spot on the platform in the shade and sat down on the ground, doing a bit of people watching before resorting to looking at my phone. The notification from the Trainline app informed me that the following train I needed to catch from Castle Cary had now been cancelled, and I'd be waiting there for over 2 hours. Brilliant!

There was a young guy on the platform a little way up from me who caught my attention. He had smart, shiny brown shoes on, but scruffy looking trousers that were too short, revealing a pair of bright white socks. On top, he had a baggy shirt. Apple Air pods poked out from his ears like oversized cotton buds, and he seemed to be subtly moving to whatever music he was listening to, repeating various patterns with his hands and feet. All 3 of my children are dancers - street dance, hip-hop, breaking, house, that sort of thing - and this guy on the platform reminded me of the subtle, nervous practicing they did before a competition or event. I wondered if he was off to battle some other dusty yutes[1] in the Badlands of Yetminster or Frome.

The train chugged into the station and I sat down in the very front carriage, which either had inadequate or broken air conditioning, and began to slowly bake. I do enjoy train travel though, and the views out the window were pretty. The countryside as we travelled on the *Heart of Wessex* line through North Dorset and into Somerset was beautiful - great fields of crops and gently sloping hills, with occasional woods spotted around.

The train guard came past and asked if I was looking to catch the train to Taunton from Castle Cary, which indeed I was. He had a bit more information on what was happening because of the previously cancelled train - as far as he knew it was being replaced by the next train through, but that would then be stopping at all the additional stops of the cancelled one. On the plus side, I wouldn't have to wait in Castle Cary for over 2 hours, but on the down side the train was going to be very busy.

A few tunnels, cuttings and level crossings later, my train came to a stop and I disembarked. Unlike Dorchester West, this station was well and truly in the 21st century with electronic information boards on the platforms, and after waiting about 5 minutes for a seemingly endless list of stations to scroll by for a train in 2 hours

---

[1] I'm absolutely totally down with the young people of today, and know all about their parlance. A "dusty yute", I am reliably informed by someone I bred, is a young person.

time it switched to the Penzance train and I found I had just 20 minutes to wait. I wandered over to the small brick shelter to get out of the direct sun.

It seems people in Castle Cary station like a drink or two. It was around midday on a Saturday, and a couple of groups of people were somewhat worse for wear. The conversation was quite sweary and about all sorts of odd things - something about an allotment, and then a wedding, and then recycling collections - but they all seemed friendly.

The Penzance train arrived and I stood at the back of the throng of people waiting to get on so as not to clout anyone with my pack. The people at my door were taking so long to get on that I gave up and walked along the platform to the next train door with no queue, stepped up and got as far as the packed vestibule before almost tripping over a teenager who was sitting on the floor. I took my hefty pack off and lowered it to the floor carefully between the teenager and a pram which poked out from the bike area into the passageway. Putting my feet either side, I balanced at a very awkward angle against the door frame. Our departure time had passed, but the train doors stood open. A woman rushed in through the door in a panic, shoving past the two women standing chatting by the door and coming to a rest next to me. She turned to face the other way. It would have been alright if she didn't have a small but very full backpack on that was jamming into me in my already uncomfortable position, but she showed no sign whatsoever of removing it. And, being me, I just stood there not saying a word.

The doors closed, but still the train just sat there not going anywhere, with a general sound of huffing, puffing and very British comments. "We're sorry for the delay, but we've had a problem closing some of the doors," came the announcement, accompanied by even more tuts, huffs, puffs and comments. Luckily, I was only on here for 20 minutes - at least once the train started moving - rather than the 5 hours to Penzance that the two women standing by the door had to look forward to.

10 minutes later the train finally got going, and we wobbled along the tracks with everyone shifting their handholds to try and stay upright. Almost everyone succeeded. There was enough time in those 20 minutes for the backpack lady next to me to get light headed and have to sit on the floor before she collapsed. We were both getting off at Taunton, and I helped her up as we approached the station, both pretty relieved to be off that train!

From the platform, I went down the steps to the subway beneath the tracks and asked the train worker for directions to the bus stop. I listened to him for a good 30 seconds, nodding in what felt like all the right places, then walked out of the station not having a clue where to go. The stop I needed turned out to be pretty much dead ahead. I'm not quite sure how he'd managed to make "it's literally outside the door" sound quite so complicated.

I put my bag against the wall behind the bus stop and settled in for the 20-minute wait, but it was quite a busy stretch of pavement so I kept moving where I'd put my pack and where to stand, so as not to have to keep moving my pack and where I was standing. Nope, that makes no sense to me either, but it's what I did.

A nervous looking man came towards the bus stop, intently scanned the timetable, crossed the road and chatted to what I can only assume was his wife. They both rushed back over, dodging between cars, and spent another few minutes looking at the timetable. I wasn't quite sure why - there were only about 3 lines of text on the whole timetable, it really wasn't over complicated. He then asked me about getting to Minehead, and I joined in having another look at the not-overly-complex timetable because it felt like the right thing to do. We both decided the right bus should probably turn up, but who really knew? Then we went back to standing in someone's way in silence.

An empty number 28 bus arrived on time, and my new bus stop acquaintance looked very relieved. Once all seated, we waited for the customary 10 minutes while no-one else got on the bus, then headed off on one of the nicest bus journeys I think I've ever been on.

It was about an hour and a quarter between Taunton and Minehead, past the Quantock hills and various bits of the West Somerset Railway. Beautiful rolling hills, old train stations and plenty of sunshine on a near empty bus… I relaxed and was now thoroughly enjoying myself.

Eventually, Minehead arrived and I jumped out. Relying on my excellent sense of direction, I walked half a mile up the road, checked my phone to see where the hotel was, then walked half a mile back to the bus stop I'd just got off at and literally across the road to the Wetherspoons Hotel that I'd booked.

You'll notice a Wetherspoons theme through this book. I don't want you to think I'm sponsored by them or some kind of huge fan, but when you're off on a self-sufficient adventure it's always nice to find something familiar, with a menu you know, where you can order on the app rather than standing at the bar with aching legs, where the prices are good and you're not going to stand out when you smell like a dead badger after walking for days on end.

The hotel was old and basic, but at £54 for the night on a flexible booking it was a bit of a bargain. The Covid pandemic had pretty much ruined travel abroad for the second year running and the world and its dog had decided to come to the West Country, so prices were skyrocketing and availability was very limited. Although I knew this in advance, it did still come back to bite me later when I found out just *how* busy and limited things were.

Food and drink wise, you know what you're going to get with a Wetherspoons, so I knew I could eat well without breaking the bank for the last night before heading off into the wilderness

Chris, my friend from university who was joining me at the start, had arranged to stay in the same hotel for this Saturday night and we would start together in the morning. I arrived at the hotel, and Chris wasn't due for a couple of hours so I thought I'd go for a bit of a wander without my pack, get some supplies for the morning and see if I could find the start of the path. It turns out that like Dorchester, Minehead also has a lovely set of gardens - Blenheim Gardens - and they were on the route to the start of the path. I seemed to be accidentally finding really nice green spaces in the middle of towns.

I reached the coast and had a look around. Ahead, across the bay were the circus-like tents of the Butlins holiday park, and to the left behind the houses and trees was a fairly substantial hill, hinting at what was to come. I turned left, and after a shorter walk than expected I found the iconic South West Coast Path start marker, a magnificent art piece depicting hands holding a map designed by 16-year-old student Sarah Ward and unveiled in 1999. I took a picture of the marker, another of the painted "South West Coast Path" on the ground, and looked up along the tarmac path that led into the not inconsiderable hills ahead. In a little over 12 hours I'd be back here, heading off into those hills, taking my first of hopefully over 1 million steps on the path.

On the way back, I passed plenty of pubs full of stag and hen parties - Minehead is pretty lively on a Saturday afternoon. The Co-op wasn't busy though, and I picked up some croissants and pain au chocolat for breakfast in the morning as we were going to start earlier than any place was likely to serve breakfast, and then headed back to chill out for a bit at the hotel.

Chris arrived later in the evening, and even though we hadn't seen each other for years - and after I got over the fact that he now seemed to have a lot more hair than I remembered, tucked into a bun on top of his head - we got chatting for an hour or so in his room. We probably would have gone on all night, discussing packs, waterproof bags, stoves and the electronics inside his hand-crafted solar-panel-battery-pack-thingy, but it was time to go and grab some dinner and carry on the conversation there.

Chris opted for the burger, I went for a steak and jacket potato, and we both had a self-imposed "2-pint limit", that covered us with another couple of hours of chatting up to 9pm at which point I suggested it might be time to get a decent night kip ready for a 6am departure in the morning.

Back in the room, I laid my morning gear out on the floor, had a shower, potentially the last one for 3 weeks. I stuck a load of gadgets on to charge, set an alarm for 5:30am and lay down in bed. The night was warm and outside the open window was some kind of extractor fan, blowing continuously and loudly. I thought it would keep me awake, but it sounded almost like a waterfall, white noise to cover the sounds from the pub below, and I fell into a decent sleep.

CHAPTER 3

Day 1: Minehead to Trentishoe

"You don't need a GPS - you can't get lost!"

-     *Comment on SWCP Facebook group*

Start Time	**6:19am**
Total Distance	**29.59 miles**
Elevation	**6,041 feet**
Total Time	**14 hours 16 mins**
Moving Time	**8 hours 57 min (18:11 min/mile)**
Steps	**63150**

Buzz. Buzz. Buzz. 5:30am. As usual when it's "Event Day" I seemed to fully wake in a split second and hit the button to shut my watch up. I jumped out of bed. OK, that's a bit of an exaggeration, but within mere minutes I was standing mostly upright. Not bad for a bloke in his mid-forties.

This was the day. Months of thinking, weeks of growing excitement, turning more recently to nervousness… and now I was here, in Minehead, on a dark Sunday morning, ready to get dressed to step out the door to walk 630 miles.

I'm more of a runner rather than a walker, so I'd opted for stuff I was comfortable wearing and knew worked for me in past events. I had trail shoes, merino wool socks, calf compression guards, lightweight gaiters, tight compression shorts covered with loose running shorts to be at least moderately dignified. On top I had a merino/polyester t-shirt and a running cap perched on the top of my head.

With everything packed, my folded poles in one hand and a little paper bag of croissants and pain-au-chocolat in the other, I headed out of the room for the last time at exactly 6am to meet Chris in the hallway. A few minutes ticked past, and just as I started to wonder if maybe he hadn't woken to his alarm, he appeared, looking a lot more sensible than me. He had a walking hat that covered the back of his neck (unlike my cap), a technical shirt that looked like a normal, smart-casual shirt, and a pair of walking trousers with hiking boots. I did wonder if maybe I'd messed up here - Chris has a lot more experience than me at walking and expeditions, and maybe hitting this in running gear was a silly idea…? But, back to my motto for the walk - "What will be, will be." I was comfortable, I was wearing things I'd tried and tested many times before and I couldn't change anything now, so I'd best just get on with it.

Before getting onto the mean streets of Minehead, we hit our first hurdle. We couldn't open the door at the front of the hotel. After a few progressively stronger yanks to the point where something felt like it might break, I figured it must be locked so we went and asked someone in the kitchen area who seemed a bit surprised to see a couple of pillocks wandering around at 6am. He said everything in the place was falling apart and broken, and you just needed to pull it hard, admirably demonstrating just that and releasing us into a grey Sunday morning.

We had a few of the French bread treats while wandering to the start point and I stuffed the rest in the pocket at the top of my backpack, a handy move I'd practiced in training so I could get things in and out of the pack without having to stop and take it off.

There was nobody around, which wasn't really surprising as it was just after 6am on a Sunday morning. We walked through the gardens and along the seafront to the start marker. There was a car parked near and some people milling around, one sat on the back of the car pulling on running shoes. They were doing the Coast-to-Coast - running a bit over 60 miles starting on the South West Coast Path then turning off through Exmoor and down to Dawlish area and the south coast. We took each other's photos at the start marker, started watches and at 6:19am we set off along the tarmac trail painted with "South West Coast Path".

The path starts on tarmac, goes along a little way through a gate onto a trail where you pass the first fingerpost sign stating "Coast Path: Minehead ¼, Poole 629¾". We walked along fairly flat ground for a while, then started going uphill. Conversation flowed, and we were enjoying the walk under the plentiful trees, glimpsing the steep drops down to the sea on our right.

30 minutes into the day, a quick glance at my GPS showed that the track we were supposed to be following was nowhere on the screen. We'd missed a turn already, despite those people on the Facebook group saying "you don't need a GPS! You can't get lost" ... Yeah? You haven't met my sense of direction. I zoomed out on the gadget, and a quick look at the map showed a path that linked our location right on the coast with the actual SWCP a bit further inland. We headed left at the small junction and began up Burgundy Chapel Combe. The problem with ending up too close to the coast in this section is that the terrain rises very sharply away from the coast as you go inland, so a quarter of a mile later we were both puffing and panting as we very slowly ascended the incredibly steep path running directly up the hill rather than gently climbing *across* the hill as we would have been doing had we taken the right path. After a fairly arduous 15 minutes, we reached the intersection with the actual coast path, took a breather and a couple of photos of the view and headed to the right.

Once back on the path we were nicely warmed up, although I was slightly concerned about my left calf muscle. For the previous couple of weeks, when I was running and walking the top of my calf had been niggling. It was nothing serious, but it was hanging around for longer than I expected. On one occasion a few years ago, I had a similar niggle and pushed a little too hard on a run and tore the muscle, leading to almost a week off any running at all. If that happened on this walk it would be game over, so I made a point of trying to really make use of my walking poles, especially on the uphill sections where I felt it the most in my calf. There was not a lot of point in worrying too much - other than trying to transfer the load to my arms more, there was nothing else I could do so I'd just have to cross my fingers and ignore it.

The terrain had changed from the tree covered path to open moorland. Despite having been technically in Exmoor National Park since soon after leaving Minehead, this was the first place that felt like how I expected Exmoor to be – moor-y. Shortly we came to the junction of the original coast path route and the newer "rugged" route. As I was aiming to cover a lot of ground each day and both were deemed official routes, I had chosen the non-rugged route on my plan and so this was the track programmed into my GPS.

We carried on over the moorland, chatting easily and then descended down from the high terrain as the coast path turned inland and we came into Bossington around 8:30, a little over 2 hours into the day. The path here was on grass, set back from the tidal marshland so as to be passable in almost all states of tide. On the right side, towards the sea, stands a line of eerie, long dead trees, looking like skeletons rising from the ground. At the end of 1996, severe storms breached the 8,000-year-old shingle barrier between the sea and the flat farmland, the salt water stripping all semblance of life from the row of trees. However, it also created a whole new ecosystem for rare plants and wildlife and was designated a Site of Special Scientific Interest in 2002.

Although flat at this point, into the distance, layers of tree covered hills dominate the horizon. Chris stopped to have a look as we passed a memorial. On 29th October 1942, a US Air Force Liberator plane had taken off in the early morning from Holmsley in Hampshire on a routine U-boat patrol mission over the Bay of Biscay. On its return journey in the afternoon, the visibility was very poor with low cloud and heavy rain, and the plane clipped the top of Bossington Hill - that we had just descended - crashing down into Porlock Marsh. Of the 12 crew on board, only 1 survived, and in 1945 the Royal British Legion erected the memorial. It was originally situated right down on the coast, but was moved in 2006 so it could be seen by more people, two of whom were now standing and contemplating the fragility of life.

45 minutes later we stopped at the Ship Inn in Porlock Weir for a coffee. Chris explained to me that this is known as the *Bottom Ship*, to distinguish it from the pub just up the road in Porlock, also called the Ship Inn.

It was nice to take the pack off my back and sit for a bit to drink coffee, but it did reveal that the bottom of the pack had been rubbing my back just around the line of my shorts on the left side, and it was a little painful. I wasn't too surprised - during training I'd had one or two walks that caused a rub in the very same area. I hadn't found a solution, but I figured as we walked I'd adjust the pack to move the load a little, swapping between shoulder and hips to try and reduce the rubbing. I was pretty accepting of it to be honest; it was a bit painful just as I took the pack off and first put it on again, but it wasn't much of an issue while walking and I hoped it would toughen up over time and become less of a problem. I did make a note to stick some Sudocrem on later to minimise the risk of any infection.

We carried on at a sensible pace for the next few hours. One of the things I was a bit worried about was that most of the training I'd done was either running or very fast walking - covering a mile in 13 or 14 minutes on flat ground. This was mostly to get the walking done quickly as my training time was limited and I figured it was better to get more miles done even if they were faster than target pace. But I was concerned that for the "real thing" I'd head off too fast and pointlessly arrive at the end of each day hours early, like I did in my long training walk to Osmington, and over time completely wear myself out. So, when I say we carried on at a "sensible pace", I mean it was quite a bit slower than the pace I had trained at... but exactly what I knew I needed to do. Don't get me wrong - we weren't going *slow*, but it felt completely sustainable to me even with the pack on my back, and I was very grateful that Chris was there to set the pace!

After Porlock Weir, we headed along a track and ended up at the Worthy Combe Toll Lodge. Built in the 19th century, the building has 2 arches - one for cars (presumably, in the past, horses) to avoid the steep Porlock Hill, and one for people to walk along the coast path. A little further along, the coast path passes through tunnels that were once part of Ashley Combe house. Built in 1799, the house became the summer retreat of Lady Ada Lovelace and her husband William King, who's family owned the house. King was an engineer with a fascination for tunnels and several were built to allow tradesmen to approach the house without disturbing residents, and one for Lady Lovelace to go down to her own private bath house unseen. Although the house was demolished in 1974 after falling into disrepair, these tunnels still remain in place on the coast path. I must admit to not knowing this information until *after* I had walked along the path. As a software engineer by trade, this is of particular interest to me as Ada Lovelace (née Byron) - daughter of the poet Lord Byron and mathematician Lady Byron - was also a superb mathematician and is often regarded as the first ever computer programmer.

20 minutes later, we rounded a corner with a junction looking down to St Beuno's church in Culbone, famous for being the smallest church in England. We took a couple of photos of the church set in a clearing against the backdrop of an impressive wooded hill, and then we headed on.

I'm not entirely sure of the exact location, but somewhere around here we met a runner coming in the other direction. As she looked up, I recognised her face as someone I followed on Instagram... I called out, asking "are you Sophie?" I was right - she stopped and we had all had a chat for a few minutes. She was running the coast path, section by section over a number of days, and she recognised me from my social media ramblings as well, knowing I was planning to cover the path in 21 days. It's amazing when you randomly connect with people you've never met before but know from a different world!

I don't think Chris and I had stopped talking since we left the hotel at 6am. General chatter about all sorts of things was going on, but at about this time Chris mentioned an incident after university that I hadn't heard about. He was surprised that I didn't know the story, so he proceeded to tell me all the details about a time around 25 years ago he'd gone mountain climbing in the Alps in France.

A group of friends had walked to a mountain hut enroute to a local summit, slept at the hut and as agreed were woken very early in the morning to continue the ascent and be able to return before the light dropped for the day. All was going well, heading into a beautiful panoramic basin with clear instructions in the guidebook saying to "avoid routes to the left." Here, they met their first problem – where did left end and right begin? They picked what looked like a decent route and headed onwards to the bottom of a climb. Two of the four had technical ice axes and crampons, while the other two (including Chris) had gear that was for rock climbing and not really suitable for ice. The group split, with one pair heading up an ice gully, and Chris and partner climbing up the rock face. Some way up, with every hand-hold yielding loose rocks and offering poor grip, Chris and his partner were beginning to regret the chosen route. They were high enough that a fall would have left them in a very bad state, but they had reached a point of no return - it was more dangerous to climb down than to continue upwards, so they had no option but to commit to the climb. Eventually they made it to the top and met with the other pair who had also had a tough time climbing up the ice that turned out to be quite unstable. In a state of euphoria at not being a broken mess at the bottom of a cliff, they all sat down with sandwiches (how British!) and pondered a few questions: Where are we? What went wrong? And how do we get down?

That part of the story is bad enough, but there was more… They agreed on a different route down, and after walking some way came to a steep downward slope. This time, they roped together and abseiled down the slope towards the glacier, each being a support for the others in case of any issues – a much safer way of descending than individually. They reached the edge of the glacier, still roped together and ready to start heading back to base across the ice.

Chris was third on the rope and in the process of putting his gloves on when the first guy stepped onto the glacier. He was technically proficient, had all the gear and plenty of idea and headed onwards. The next guy onto the ice was less confident, and within a few steps he fell and began sliding down the ice, at which point all hell broke loose…

The leader read the situation, and quickly stuck his axes and crampons into the ice to arrest the slide. As the second guy slid down the ice, the rope to Chris suddenly pulled, who at this point was midway through donning gloves. He wasn't expecting a sudden and powerful jerk on the rope and was pulled of his feet, bashing his hip on a rock and hitting his head so hard that he lost consciousness despite his helmet and began sliding down on the ice. Meanwhile, the last guy on the rope was behind a jutting rock pinnacle, bracing to take the sudden weight of between 2 and 3 people through his harness – a situation that had a high potential of massive injury or even death. Suddenly, the rope caught on another pinnacle of rock, taking the strain and stopping the slide. A genuinely miraculous escape – it turned out that at the bottom of the rope, the lowest person was only metres from a crevasse in the glacier!

Chris regained consciousness and they managed to get down off the ice. One of the pair with ice crampons was kicking footholds in the ground for Chris to use as he was in a bad way and walking was difficulty, but this continuous kicking stripped skin from shins and ended up with 2 people who couldn't walk well! The decision was made that the uninjured pair would go back to the mountain hut to check in and avoid a massive charge for a mountain rescue helicopter search, while the injured pair would head straight back to the campsite. After a gruelling 8 mile walk taking 5 hours, Chris and his partner arrived back at the campsite after dark.

Apparently, the cure for almost dying on a glacier is copious amounts of beer - none of them sought medical attention, but within a few days they were back up on the mountains again. Nutcases!

Back to the safety of Britain's longest national trail, where the biggest risk is… well, I suppose falling off a cliff. But I was hoping that wouldn't happen!

At 11:35am, unbeknownst to us, we crossed a stream and passed from Somerset into Devon, and shortly after we stopped at Sister's Fountain. Erected in the 19th century, it consists of an arch of coarse stone rubble forming a chamber covering a bubbling spring, with a stone cross on the top. It was named after the nieces of the owner of the estate at the time, but the spring itself is the subject of legend. It's said that Jesus drank here as a youth on his way to Glastonbury. I'm not sure I believe the story - I really don't think the Glastonbury Festival has been going for that long (…I'll get my coat).

For quite some time, the path had been under the cover of trees with only occasional views of the sea through the branches. You could believe you were in a deep inland forest, rather than within a few metres of cliffs down to the coast. Later through gaps in the woods, there were views of The Foreland in the distance, and soon we were walking up a hill with impressive views of the huge shingle-clad hill of Coddow Combe that ran towards Foreland Point.

We tipped over the summit of Contisbury hill and walked along a quite exposed stretch, the path itself flat and wide enough to walk on, but to the right was a steep slippery looking grass slope that ran down to a cliff edge and disappeared into the sea beyond - you wouldn't want to slip off here! We continued down into the town of Lynmouth and arrived just as the mist that had been floating on the hills most of the morning had burnt off, turning the day into a sunny, moderately hot one.

Lynmouth was the first proper town we'd got to since leaving Minehead, and it was full of people. We crossed the bridge over the West Lyn River and headed into the town where there were plenty of places to get food. Being around 2pm, lunch was long overdue so we called into a fish and chip shop, ordered a couple of portions of battered sausage and chips and sat inside to eat. After finishing, walking down the road we passed a cafe selling ice-cream. Chris has a bit of a thing for ice-cream, and being from Somerset he knows his stuff when it comes to the various West Country dairies. I bowed to his expertise and copied his order, ending up with a really delicious honey and stem-ginger ice-cream cone.

All in, we stopped for just about an hour before moving on again. It was time to top up water bottles, and I fired up the very useful *Refill* app on my phone which shows a map of all the places happy to refill water for you. The nearest spot was the Memorial

Hall just along the road, a memorial to the catastrophic floods of almost 70 years before.

On the night of the 15th August 1952, a tropical storm broke over south-west England, depositing a huge amount of water onto the already saturated land of Exmoor. Debris-laden flood waters cascaded down the river towards the village of Lynmouth, but just outside the village the debris formed a dam, holding back an ever-growing mass of water. After a time, the dam broke sending the deluge, boulders and trees into the village. More than 100 buildings were destroyed, 28 of the 31 bridges washed away and 34 people lost their lives along with another 420 being made homeless. The Memorial Hall in Lynmouth houses a permanent exhibition with a pre-flood scale model and details of the destroyed buildings and how to find them. We didn't have time to go on a building tour, but we topped up our water bottles with cold filtered water from the *Refill* station outside then carried on round to the bottom station of the Lynmouth-Lynton Cliff railway.

On the sea front is an eye-catching statue called The Walker, designed by Richard Graham to symbolise walkers on the Coleridge way. Constructed from rods of metal, it depicts a man with a walking stick, cap and outstretched hand intended for you to shake while having your photo taken. It's been installed where the Coleridge Way, Two Moors Way, South West Coast Path and Tarka Trail meet to promote Lynmouth as a key point for walkers. We both took a good look at the statue, but it was in a busy area and surrounded by people so we didn't wait around to get the classic "handshake" photo.

Then… we went up. I knew the hill between Lynmouth and Lynton was a bit legendary, but I figured it wouldn't be particularly long. I was wrong. The cliff railway is a proper bit of engineering and goes up about 500ft at a gradient of almost 60% with the path zig-zagging either side to get those silly enough to walk it to the top!

Opened in 1890, the cars are powered by the weight of water, which is piped over a mile from the river and fills a 3000-litre tank in the top car. When enough water is added, the car descends to the bottom where the water is emptied and the top car filled again. The height combined with its propulsion mechanism wins it the accolade of the world's highest and steepest water-powered railway. It's brilliant - so simple, and has been running for over 130 years.

The path zig-zags up the hill, and after a fair amount of walking up an impressively steep path, you cross a bridge over the track… to realise you're now about ⅓ of the way up. Continuing on up, the second bridge crosses still below the half-way point, identified by the widening of the pair of tracks to let the upward and downward trains pass. Still further up, over another bridge and you're nearing the top. Looking down gives a real vertigo-inducing sense of the steepness of the track. Carry on, and eventually you're at the top.

Half an hour out of Lynton, walking along a flat tarmac path cut along a fairly steep slope down to the sea, we entered the

Valley of Rocks (also known as Valley of the Rocks - both appear to be equally valid). This U-shaped valley runs parallel to the coast with epic granite stone formations to the seaward side. Given its shape, it would be expected that this valley was formed by a glacier, but that doesn't seem to be the case. There are theories that it was formed by either the river flowing through, or by a lake formed when the river was blocked by a glacier, but the exact cause of the unique geology of the area is still a bit of mystery.

The Valley of Rocks is also well known for feral goats which are often seen balancing precariously on the granite peaks and cliffs, but we didn't see any goats in the area at all on that day. Maybe they don't like being out in the sunshine? I took a few photos of Chris standing on various edges with big drops and sea behind, and we admired the look of the whole place, peaks rising up with names like *Rugged Jack*, *Castle Rock* and *The White Lady* dominant against the skyline.

After Valley of Rocks, we soon passed the edge of Lee Abbey, home to a Christian community. This may explain why the £2 charge for using the toll road by car appeared to be an honesty box, it seemed strangely trusting as we passed by and took the footpath to the left. We continued along a narrow path by fields, up some steps and then there were some road sections. Turning off the road, we passed the back of Lee Bay, round Crock Point and then the trail went into a high wooded area above the sea at Woody Bay which had a rain-forest feel to it.

At 5:30pm, a few hours after leaving Lynton, we rounded the final corner away from the coast heading into the valley at Heddon's Mouth. The deep valley dropped away to the sea, and on the far side a small stone building stood which I thought might be a lime kiln although I'd never (knowingly) seen one before. Limestone arrived on land aboard ships, but transporting limestone on land was difficult in the pre-industrial era. Coastal lime kilns were used to heat the mineral to around 1000°C and produce lime - the useful end product - which was then directly sold on for agricultural use and as a building material. By the late 19th century, it became cheaper to crush the lime mechanically so the kilns fell out of use and many are now just piles of rocks or ruins. The kiln at Heddon's Mouth was restored by the National Trust in 1982 and is subsequently protected from the sea by a boulder wall built in 1992. In the orange glow of the evening sunlight, it was just another hint at the tremendous history associated on this path.

Our plan had always been to go to the Hunter's Inn just inland from Heddon's Mouth to get some dinner and we were very much looking forward to it after our first long day. At the bottom of the valley, a finger-post sign showed the coast path continuing across a little bridge to the west, with the pub ½ mile further inland to the south. We were both a bit worn out from walking and the slight uphill path seemed to take longer and was harder than expected, but eventually we walked through the garden at the back of the pub, resisted the urge to play on the wooden snakes and carried on round to the front which was laid out with mostly empty benches with parasols.

It was at this point that it occurred to us that potentially there might not be space for dinner, and after a quick chat with the bar staff it transpired that they were short staffed and were limiting the number of covers so were therefore fully booked. Back to my motto for this adventure: "It is what it is", and although a bit disappointed we got our first beers of the walk and sat down on one of the outdoor tables for a bit to relax. We had an hour or so there, chatting and making good use of the decent Wi-Fi. It was warm, the light was beautiful and we were enjoying just chilling for a bit, so had another pint and carried on chatting for a while longer before deciding it was probably time to get back to the coast path before it got too dark.

We returned to that little bridge and started heading up the substantial hill on the other side of the valley to what would hopefully be a great spot for wild camping. It was a fairly tough climb, zig-zagging up the steep side of the valley. Some particularly steep sections were on orange gravel with our feet slipping back often, but walking poles, the conversation and the warm feel from a couple of beers certainly helped distract from the effort. Once over the top, the terrain became a lot flatter, albeit with all 1,043ft of Great Hangman - the highest point on the whole South West Coast Path - in the middle distance.

The sun was on its way down below the horizon and although it was getting darker, I wasn't concerned, more interested in Chris's opinions on various places to camp. We found what looked like a great potential spot on the top of a small hill just inland from the path on some access land, but when we went up to look, we found there were already about 6 tents pitched on the spot and decided not to crash the party but to move on a bit.

We walked for another 5 minutes or so, commenting on a field ahead that had a few tents set up pretty much in the middle. It seemed a bit indiscreet - we figured they were wild camping and people were just being a bit brazen at this time. There had been plenty of recent news reports of people camping in spots that were either dangerous like on the edge of cliffs, or just plain inconsiderate. As we approached the corner of that field, we saw the coast path route went across a style and through the field. We didn't cross the style as a patch of land on the seaward side of the fence had caught our eye so we went to have a look.

It was a little dicey, having to step across a narrow bit of ground with quite a significant drop to the right, but it opened up to an area that would have been fine for 2 small tents and was away from the drop. What wasn't ideal, however, was the brambles and mole hills all over the ground, and also how visible we would be from the land. In an absolute emergency it would have sufficed, but we decided to go back and carry on along the path as there would still be light for another 30 minutes or so and after that we had head torches.

We stepped back across the narrow gap, then over the style and there, unmissable against the fence was a white wooden board. It said "Camping", and underneath there was a mobile number. It was - quite literally - a sign!

Moments later I was chatting to the owner and we had 2 spots at £5 each which they trusted us to leave in a box in the shed on the site. Both very grateful, we headed into the field to find a flat spot. 30 seconds later my phone rang - they guy just wanted to let us know that the site even had toilets and showers in the buildings at the bottom of the field, and bottled water in the box in the middle. By this point it was dark enough not to really be able to make them out, but I was surprised. Despite being just a field, these people had put some effort in to make it a decent spot to camp. On our first night, we'd fallen on our feet. A campsite had magically appeared just where we needed it. I hoped this was a sign of things to come.

It took longer than I expected to get set up for the first time. There was light in the sky but not really enough to comfortably get a tent fully constructed and it had noticeably darkened even as we'd walked the short distance from the style to our spot. Head torches on, tent out the bag, I got some pegs in the ground and with the aid of my walking pole produced an impressive erection (I'm such a child!). Next it was the inflatable mat out, which I made fairly light work of with the inflation bag. In case you don't know, some sleeping mats come with a bag you use to help with inflation. Essentially, it's an air-tight bag that clips to the mat valve at one end, and has a big, wide opening at the other end. You blow into the open end from a distance, and with one or two gentle breaths the bag opens right up, like you're blowing into an open bin bag, filling with a lot more air than you're breathing out. You then fold over the top to seal and squeeze that full bag of air into the mat. The end result is it requires a couple of gentle breaths, 4 or 5 times, to inflate the whole mat - rather than 5 minutes of continuous blowing directly into the mat and several episodes of light-headedness like with any other one I've had! I hadn't used an inflation bag before I had this mat, and I'd almost not bothered with it for this trip, but it turned out to be incredibly useful.

While I was faffing with my tent and mat, Chris had got his stove on for some noodles for dinner. I opened my luxury meal: a 200g bag of salt and vinegar peanuts I'd been carrying since I left home. It wasn't ideal, but it did have a lot of calories and protein so I was hoping my body could do something useful with it overnight and get me in a fit state for another day tomorrow.

We both finished setting up, had a look around each other's tents having now seen them set up for the first time, and by around 9:30pm I was zipped into my tent, changing out of the clothes I'd worn all day and into the clean ones to wear for tomorrow. I remembered to rub Sudocrem into the now raw and inflamed section of my lower back where the bag had been continually rubbing, and settled down onto the air mat, my sleeping bag resting on top of me as it was too hot to be inside. Laying down was a very, very pleasant feeling after walking 30 miles with 6,000ft of climb, and despite some restlessness in my legs and feet from the long day it didn't take long to fall into a recuperative sleep.

CHAPTER 4

Day 2: Trentishoe to Braunton

"Don't Panic!"

- *Douglas Adams*

Start Time	**6:54am**
Total Distance	**36.66 miles**
Elevation	**5,331 feet**
Total Time	**13 hours 45 minutes**
Moving Time	**9 hours 50 minutes (16:57 min/mi)**
Steps	**74382**

I'm not very good at sleeping in a tent. When we used to go camping in a big family tent, I would describe my sleep as… crap. We eventually invested in a massive, heavy and thick inflatable double mattress, and that upgraded it to… rubbish.

For the months before leaving on the SWCP I tried about 10 times with various tents and mats and always had a pretty disturbed sleep, even after being tired from walking for a full day. To be fair, quite a few of those bad nights during the previous year were down to either an inadequate sleeping bag or a very slippery sleeping mat, but let's just say I wasn't expecting much in the sleep department and was as prepared as I could be to expect tiredness.

But on this night in Trentishoe, I had a decent sleep. It wasn't perfect - a long way from a typical night in bed - with quite a bit of rolling around, getting in and out of the sleeping bag as the night cooled, and restless legs from all the walking. But on the whole I slept for a fair chunk of the night and woke to the alarm at 5:50am feeling actually quite refreshed and ready to go.

It's amazing how much mending your body can do overnight. As I lay on the mat before falling asleep last night, my legs felt tight and tingly, uncomfortably worn from the stress of a day of walking. But as the sun hinted at coming up over the hill on that morning, they felt like new again. Which was good, considering what I had planned for them.

While my legs were feeling good and my head was beginning to join the land of the living, there was a small issue: dew. The air during the day was warm, holding lots of moisture. At night when it cooled down, the trapped water vapour condensed on... everything. The grass was very wet outside as if it had been raining, and the inside and outside of the tent flysheet was literally dripping. I managed to pack up my airbed, sleeping bag and get my socks and shoes on while inside the tent, carefully avoiding touching the outside by sitting in the tallest point in the centre with my back to the walking pole. I then opened up the outer door and threw the fabric back on to the top of the tent and crawled out to see what the day had to offer. The wind blew, and the dripping wet door-section landed flat on my back. I didn't swear *too* much as the chill soaked through my clean, once-dry top.

The sun wasn't going to bother getting up for at least another 20 minutes, but anyone who's tried to take sunrise photos knows that the show starts early. Looking back the way we'd come from last night, the sky ranged from a fiery orange through to deep blue, with contrasting dark clouds in shadow above Highveer Point. In the other direction, the hills were bathed in a beautiful pink light. It's always a privilege to be awake around sunrise, and this day didn't disappoint.

My pack, shoes and a few drybags were sitting on top of a small square of polycro - the plastic sheeting used as secondary double-glazing, a pack of which I'd bought from Amazon before leaving. For under £10 I bought enough to line a small field with, cut some sections and stuffed them in my pack in case they came in handy. They did. Polycro is lightweight, folds small and is resistant to sharp things like brambles and thorns, so was ideal to stop any kit that would potentially have to lay on wet ground from getting soaked or damaged. I dragged the loaded sheet out and started working on packing things back away.

I pulled the pegs out of the ground, collapsing the tent in an untidy heap. After rescuing my walking pole, I gave the whole tent a jolly good shake, covering my legs and shoes with water in the process, then proceeded to squash it into the sack. It's amazing how compact that little tent can be - I felt like Mary Poppins shoving handful after handful of soggy, wet tent material into that small bag, and it just kept going. Once in, a good squash pumped some of the excess water out through the sides of the (obviously not waterproof) sack, but it was still considerably wetter and heavier than the dry tent of the day before. I dug around in my pack and found a plastic bag which wasn't being used and put the tent inside to minimise the amount of water let loose inside my pack. I was expecting to notice the extra weight of the water, but in reality, once we got going the bag felt pretty much identical to the previous day. That was something I learnt over the trip - despite being told every gram counts and picking lightweight kit, when your bag weighs 12 or 13kg, adding another kilogram or two really doesn't make much of a difference. At least that's how it felt to me with the pack I had.

Based on previous experience, I wasn't surprised that once everything was packed away and we were up and ready, I wasn't exactly raring to go. I'd walked 30 miles with 12-13kg on my back the day before, with a considerable amount of climbing. I wasn't used to sleeping in a tent, and I was about to head out for another full day - a day that was planned to be a bit longer. The thing is… just knowing that I might not feel great right now - having experienced it in the past and got past it - meant I could just chill and not overthink it. Yeah, I don't feel great *now*, but that doesn't mean I won't in an hour or two. *Now* I feel tired, but today could be the best day *ever!*

I didn't have anything in my pack that would have worked as a breakfast, but I did have some chocolate covered espresso beans that Eva had got me before leaving. She bought me them as a gift, in their big, heavy, cardboard tube (every gram counts!), and I thought "Oh no, that's a load of weight I don't need to be carrying." But I'm a sentimental sod, and the fact that they were a gift specifically for the trip meant I had to take them, so I shrunk them down as much as possible, stripping off the cardboard tube and putting them in a plastic bag in the middle of my pack. And then, on that first morning of waking up out in the world, they were… perfect! They served both as calories and caffeine, and they worked an absolute treat as an alternative to a cup of coffee. Once again, my wife had accidentally[2] foreseen my need for something that at the time I thought would just be useless extra weight.

---

[2] She does this far too often for it to be accidental. I reckon she's got some sort of time machine, but she's being very cagey about it.

We set off out the field just before 7am with packs and full bottles of water. There was no running water at the site, but in the middle of the field was a plastic box filled with about twenty 2 litre bottles of fresh water, so I'd filled my bottles and Chris his pack bladder from them as we passed.

It was supposed to be about 4 miles to Combe Martin. Between us and breakfast was Great Hangman - the highest point on the whole of the South West Coast Path. As I hoped, my lull after packing the tent away had gone, my spirit was improving rapidly and my legs were feeling good after the first mile or so, but Chris was obviously quite tired from the day before and moving pretty slowly. Again though, I was glad to not be charging off at super-speed at the start, but I did want to be moving a little quicker than this once we got some food in and were on better ground.

A little way along from the campsite, we were treated to the view of clear landscape ahead, with the cliff heading down to the sea covered in a layer of sea mist. It looked like the land was rising out of the clouds, the sea wasn't even visible except right out towards the horizon. I've seen pictures from the top of mountains that look like that, but never expected to see a jaw-dropping sight like this on day 2 of my coast path wander. The recipe for magic: early or late sunlight, add some steep drops to the pot, throw in a bit of low-level fog and a helping of luck and you're on to a winner!

We dropped into the valley at Sherrycombe to a height of around 140m (460ft), and then began the climb to the full 318m

(1,043 feet) to the top of Great Hangman. At the seaward end of the valley, the mist was flowing in and the view behind us was absolutely stunning as the sun rose and bathed everything in golden morning light.

I did notice - or rather, I noticed that I *didn't* notice - my calf muscle. It had been a concern yesterday morning, but this morning climbing some significant hills, it felt fine. Normal. Exactly like the other one. That was really promising: instead of breaking after 30 miles and 6,000ft of climb the day before, I was actually mending.

You can't miss the cairn announcing the top of Great Hangman - a huge pile of stones, with lots of little stacks of pebbles balanced on top. Here we were, higher than we had been, and higher than we were going to be. Nowhere else along the whole 630 miles of coast path was as high as this point. The early morning sunshine lit the scenery in beautiful golden yellow, and the sea mist hung like a shroud to the lower cliffs.

We followed the path to Little Hangman, around ⅔ the height of Great Hangman at 100 metres lower, then down what seemed like endless narrow, winding paths with no sea view. At a little after 9am and close to 6 miles after leaving our campsite, we arrived in Combe Martin.

I'd had my heart set on getting a nice full English breakfast here, but it soon became apparent that not a lot was open at 9am on a Monday morning. I didn't realise it yet, but the logistics of food and sleep were the critical component of this adventure, and I didn't get it all right. We walked up and down the road looking in the windows of various places, but the only option we found for a full breakfast wouldn't be opening for another hour. A bit disappointed, I settled for a coffee and breakfast bap from the Castaway Cafe on the main street.

With our coffees in hand, we took a seat on the last outside table and I walked the short distance back to the counter to get the baps, the first time without my pack on for a day or so. It was a very odd feeling - I felt lighter than air, like balloons were pulling me up and making every step feel like a bounce! I wondered if this feeling would continue on after I'd finished the walk - it would be quite nice if every step felt as easy as if I was bouncing in space, walking and running becoming a doddle... I wasn't convinced it would last though.

I'm going to take a moment here and say something that I'm probably going to repeat through this, but I find it interesting. The world we live in now - at least for me, living in the south of England and having enough disposable income - has everything you want. Fancy a pizza? - order one. A curry? - nip down the takeaway. Beer? - Tesco's is open. A snack? - pop to the shop around the corner. We've got everything. On tap. Whenever you want. And one thing I was starting to realise was here, now, on my adventure it wasn't going to work like that. I had the means, but the £10 in your pocket is useless if you're hungry or thirsty on a path 5 miles from anywhere. I was going to need to do that thing my wife does so well and I'm absolutely crap at: forward planning.

The baps were ready, and back at our table we tucked in - egg, bacon and sausage in a decent sized and nicely soft bread roll. They went down a treat and along with the coffee, and I felt fully human again.

When finished, we crossed the road and called into the local Premier store. I got a drink, so that I could have something other than water. I know water is essential, but it's so *boring* - don't underestimate the mental stimulation of… well, *anything* else! I also bought a packet of crisps and a chicken tikka slice to stick in the top of my bag to eat later - there we go, forward planning in action! Chris bought a pack of plasters to sort out an issue caused by his shirt trying to remove his nipples from his chest sometime during the 30 miles of walking yesterday.

You know a while back I was writing about feeling a bit incorrectly dressed as we left Minehead, a bit inexperienced, like wearing "running stuff" was wrong and Chris had it right? I'm not saying anything bad about Chris's choices because they seemed very sensible, but something I may have done more than him was to try out every bit of kit I took with me on more than one occasion during training. I may sound picky with my kit choices in various places in this book, but it's usually because I found a problem with something else, and that problem was found when I tried things out. Something rubbed, something else didn't fit, another thing just got in the way. And something unexpected was a bloody lifesaver. Like chocolate covered coffee beans… although I can't take credit for that one.

Out of Combe Martin we passed the sign which gave some indication of what we'd done so far: "Coast Path: Poole 595, Minehead 35". Next stop, Ilfracombe. We walked a little way along a path, then uphill on the pavement of a road before turning back towards the coast. We stopped to check the route when faced with 3 paths going in more-or-less the same direction, but picked the right one - the Old Coast Road (yes, there's a clue in the name, but you can't assume anything in the South West!)

The path went through a campsite which we both admired a little enviously, thinking about how nice it would be to be somewhere like this at the end of the day. On the path a little further along we stopped on a bench by a sign against a tree. It shouted: "Voted the happiest view in the UK!". If the UK is a big fan of grey, it was probably right. In front was a steep drop that was almost entirely filled with fog, making it difficult to even make out the beach below. Behind me, Chris was trying to subtly stick plasters to his nipples when a woman walking a dog appeared. Those are the rules - if you stop to stick plaster to your nipples, a woman walking a dog will appear out of thin air. We chatted for a bit. She didn't mention Chris's nipples, which was good. Where she'd just come from a few minutes before had no fog at all and was bathed in full sunshine, but here we were under the fairly thick fog, blocking the sun from view. I was quite glad really, I'm sure there was plenty of heat to come later in the day, but the longer it held off the better as far as I was concerned - my back was already sweaty enough.

The path continued along through woods and next to roads until dropping down to Hele Bay, pretty near to Ilfracombe now. The path went into a park area and up an unexpectedly steep hill, climbing from sea level to 400ft along a series of zigzags which both surprised and wore us out. A sign halfway up showed the promised great views over Ilfracombe, but as we got to the top and had a chance of seeing down, again the whole place was shrouded in a layer of fog. The picture board might as well have shown a grey square.

We continued down the steep hill into Ilfracombe, passing a few distinctive people on the way down. We stopped at the skate park for Chris to empty something out of his shoe, continued on to the edge of a building site, fences blocking the path and a very unclear diversion which seemed to be signed in two opposing directions. We ended up walking around past a large water treatment plant, which obviously turned out to be the wrong way, as once we managed to get back on to the path we then had to again pass the same people we'd previously walked past coming down the hill. Another navigation cock-up by the man with the GPS strapped to his bag. I thank you! [takes a bow].

Walking along the quay area of Ilfracombe we got chatting with a couple of women who were walking the path with relatively small day packs, having their luggage transported to the end point each day - that seemed like a much more sensible idea! As usual, the concept of completing the whole path in 21 days with everything in your pack seemed to them like an astounding - and I'm pretty sure, ridiculous - idea.

Rounding the corner onto the main street along the quay, we walked along to try and find a pub or somewhere to get a sit-down meal. We did find a pub at the end, but it was closed due to staff shortage or some other Covid related issue (bloody 2021!), so we decided to walk back and get something from one of the many food outlets on the street. Chris settled on a slice of pizza and I carried on down to the pasty shop, again meeting and chatting with the two women doing the daily walks as we waited. I met Chris back on a seat on the quay wall and we tucked into pizza, pasty and coffee to refuel. It was 12:30pm, and the fog was getting lighter and more patchy as it hung over the harbour.

The street was very busy and being quite narrow there were a lot of lorries, caravans, motorhomes and cars fighting for passage along the narrow sections, making a lot of noise and generally causing chaos. It was full of fumes and the vehicles would come quite close to us as they passed each other, not the most pleasant lunch spot but on the plus side behind us was the low-tide, boat-filled harbour with the fog in the distance catching the sunlight in a slightly ethereal way. And at least we could sit and eat and not be walking for a bit which was a welcome break.

It was at this point that we discussed progress. We were dropping behind my original plan and at the current speed would have to stop a good few miles early. Chris was feeling generally OK but not in a position to speed up to my originally planned walking pace for the day, but I felt good, happy to head on a bit faster. In our planning for this walk, we had decided on "Top

Gear Rules" - if one of us wanted to head on, we would. So, with some trepidation, I proposed a split.

Chris wasn't so interested in doing every step of the SWCP and was happy to cut a few corners here and there, so we decided I'd go on from Ilfracombe and at some point over the next hours or days he'd get ahead and we'd meet up again.

We stuck together after eating our food, walking down to the toilets at the end of the harbour and refilling bottles in a cafe. The staff were pleasant in the cafe, but the customers arriving as we left were very rude, demanding quick service as they were "fed up". I'd seen reports of this in the media - places in Cornwall especially were understaffed due to Covid, and customers were getting grumpy about the lack of service - but I wasn't expecting to see it quite as blatantly as this idiot being so rude to the waitress. I *almost* turned back and had a word with the guy to tell him to be more polite, but for one reason or another I let it go with just a "good luck" and smile to the waitress who, to be honest, looked like she was used to it and was about to unleash hell on the twat!

At the end of the prominent harbour wall is a big statue called *Verity*. It's a huge piece, standing over 20 metres tall and depicting a pregnant woman holding a sword and the scales of justice while standing on a pile of law books. From one side, her internal anatomy is visible clearly showing the foetus, making it somewhat controversial and bringing the tourists flocking. Obviously, with it being so tall and unmissable, I completely missed it. Sorry Damian Hurst, you're going to have to make something bigger to get my attention next time.

Chris and I walked together back out the harbour and along the path round Capstone Hill and to the Jubilee Gardens in town. We decided it would be far more fun to walk to the end of the car park than along the coast path. Turning at the end with the grace and elegance of a pair of graceful and elegant things who hadn't just gone the wrong way, we walked back past the odd conical building which I commented on reminding me a little of the Hexagon theatre in Reading. We didn't find out what it was at the time, but I've since learnt that the building is also a theatre. Built in the 1980's to replace The Pavilion theatre which was partially destroyed by fire, this was the Landmark Theatre - or locally "Madonna's Bra" due to its double-cone design.

After not a great deal of hunting around, we found the correct path and headed on the road uphill out of the town at 1:30pm. The difference in our pace was more apparent on the hills, so Chris and I said our goodbyes for the time being and I headed off up the hill on my own.

The path quickly lost the town feel and I was quite glad. I like my coast path to… well, ideally, have no other people about! Generally this meant rough trails and lovely views instead of busy towns. Soon, I was on a quiet road that went down. And down. And down some more. And then 30 minutes outside of Ilfracombe I was walking across the back of Lee Bay with a slight sense of déjà vu…

One thing I've learnt while researching place names in the West Country is that there are certain names that are reused a lot - Lee Bay, Pentire Point, Lo(o)e, Seato(w)n. They mean things like "promontory" or "vegetation covered area", but they're not particularly specific so back in the olden-days, Bob in Cornwall used the same name as Fred in Devon when they drew the map. It can get quite confusing if you don't specify the general area, or at least the county!

This was Lee Bay just past Ilfracombe, rather than Lee Bay a little west of Lynton. And it was absolutely beautiful. The sun shone on the grey granite rocks which stood highlighted against the grey fog still hanging out to sea. The ground was rounded granite boulders on one side of a concrete walkway running out to sea, and covered with brown seaweed on the other side. The whole bay looked oddly low-contrast and grey. It was stunning.

As I walked up the steep road hill out of Lee Bay, I caught part of a conversation behind me. A man had run over to talk to the driver of a Jaguar XK who was waiting to turn left out onto the road I was walking along to explain that it was a really, really bad idea for him to go that way due to it being incredibly narrow, steep and twisty. I don't know if he heeded the warning as shortly after I turned off the road and continued on a steep footpath, but from what I saw at the start of the road I wouldn't like to have been driving up it.

I passed a very sweet bridge over a dry stream bed. There were a couple of stone steps up to the small wooden bridge which met the far bank at a manmade dry-stone shelf of tightly packed slim granite stones. The path went on to a small gate which led onto the fern covered hill and disappeared into the fog. Towards the sea, there were some large pieces of driftwood, laid out like sculptures. To me at that point, the whole scene was just wonderfully idyllic and I stopped a moment to take a few photos.

Five minutes more up the hill I was just above Bull Point lighthouse, it's top like a white helmet poking up out of the mist. The original lighthouse was built in 1879, but suffered damage in 1972 when the ground it was situated on subsided. The lighthouse today was constructed in 1974 and stands 11 metres tall above the ground level at the top of the cliff.

The path was quite undulating without having any particularly big hills, and the fog was clearing revealing a really amazing view. The landscape was rough, rugged and the shelf-like rock formations down towards the sea were amazing. I was enjoying looking out to sea so much I ended up taking a wrong turn by a group of people on the path, and heading inland towards Mortehoe before fairly quickly realising the views were disappearing and being replaced by some buildings in the distance. A quick glance at my GPS showed where I'd gone wrong and I was back on the track in 2 minutes - walking past the same people - on my way to Morte Point.

Morte Point, which translates as *death point*, is a notorious headland that has been the site of many shipwrecks. In the winter of 1852 alone, five ships were wrecked here, one carrying a cargo of live pigs. Most of the pigs survived and colonised the nearby beach, so the area just south of the point is named *Grunta Beach*.

When I rounded Morte Point at a little after 3pm, I got my first view of Woolacombe sands stretching for 2 miles[3] along the coast. The last few miles of path and the road led me into the town, ready to stop for a bit. Once on the road section, I checked my *Refill* app for water suppliers and found the Tourist Information Centre a little way down the road. I called in and sure enough they were happy to top the bottles up and I headed further into town.

I'd been warned to avoid Woolacombe as it was very busy, but I needed some food so headed slightly inland towards the obvious food places along West Road. I skipped the fish & chip shop on the corner which had a queue coming out the door and down the steps, and settled on the Captain's Table Cafe at the far end of the road. After covering around 50 miles and not having had much in the way of a wash for over 36 hours I probably smelt like a rotting ferret, so I took a seat outside so as not to clear the restaurant. This quickly turned out to be a bad idea - the direct sunlight was baking me alive, so I went inside and sat on a seat by the window looking out at the world.

I do love a burger and chips and all that sort of unhealthy food as an occasional treat, and I was certainly earning it with the walking distance I was doing at the moment. But when I stopped, I had a real urge for something a bit more wholesome, so ordered

---

[3] There are a lot of reports of the beach being 3 miles, but Wikipedia stated the 3 miles was incorrect and it was actually 2 miles. I measured it on a map and it came out as 2.1 miles.

a jacket potato with cheese and beans and salad. I couldn't pass up the opportunity to have a pint Korev (a jolly nice Cornish lager) too - all that sunshine pretty much demanded it! That's the nice thing about walking rather than running - you can do things like have a decent meal and a beer and it doesn't give you a stitch or slow you down significantly as long as you don't go completely over the top. If anything, missing out on the food (and I'm going to argue the beer as well!) will be the thing to slow you down as you get tired.

After paying the bill, I headed upstairs to the toilet and took the opportunity to wash my face. Having not done it for nearly 2 days, it's funny how simple things take on a whole new feeling. It was absolutely lush! Soapy, warm water and a squeaky-clean face just felt so nice.

I'd been pretty efficient with eating, taking just 30 minutes from finding the cafe to leaving, nicely satiated. I headed off back down to the beach and took a left through the car park. I realise now that the actual path went slightly to the right of where I walked, along the top of the beach, but I was following a GPS track laid down by Kristian Morgan (who as I mentioned before has the record for the SWCP), and I figured if it was good enough for him, it's good enough for me.

A couple of miles of slightly uphill car park on Marine Drive was a bit dull though. I took the opportunity to dig out my MP3 player. Rather than using my phone, for long events I've had a cheap MP3 player that doesn't have any fancy features but lasts for something like 85 hours on a single charge. I generally put one headphone in with an album on loop or the whole collection on shuffle, quietly playing in the background rather than blasting music into both ears. In that way, I can still hear the environment: birds, wind in the trees, waves on the beach or rocks, and can also stay safe hearing cars and have conversations with people I pass. I clicked through the albums and settled on *Final Straw* from *Snow Patrol*.

At the top of the extraordinarily long car parking area of Marine Drive, I was back onto a trail and met up with the correct SWCP route. I knew from my planning that this day wasn't particularly hilly after dropping down from Great Hangman and into Combe Martin earlier that morning. There was some undulation through the day but it wasn't overly taxing, and as I went round Baggy Point at around 5:30pm, I knew I had finished all of the significant hills for about the next 30 miles, until the far side of Westward Ho!

On the outskirts of Croyde I called in to the Baggy Point car park and cafe to try and find some water. Even though it was early evening, the sun was still beating down and in the heat I was drinking quite a lot. But it was almost 6pm, and the cafe was closed. I had a look around for an outside tap, but couldn't find anything so continued on.

Croyde is a renowned surfing beach which looked lovely as I approached it from Baggy Point, but as I turned the corner heading south I realised with a certain amount of horror that the path went on to the soft, smooth, lovely-to-look-at-but-horrible-to-walk-on sand. I wasn't sure how far it went, but I had visions of endless trudging and my shoes filling up with sand, then having to strip off 18 layers of nonsense on my legs to get to them and empty out half a beach that found its way into my socks.

As it turns out I needn't have worried. The gaiters I had on did their job perfectly - as far as I could tell, not a single grain of sand ended up in my shoes! Walking on the sand felt like hard work though. I'd just passed 27 miles so far that day and the plan still had me doing another 5 more. After following the sand inland and crossing a stream, I headed to the far end of the beach past a guy filming the warm up for some kind of surfing event out to sea. I followed the majority of people over some rocks, up some steps and I was glad to get back on to a more solid path. I sent a text message to Chris, partly to guide him in the right direction, and partly to warn him about the sand section.

There was a small cafe just by the main road, so I left the path and headed straight for it to fill up my water bottles. They were happy to fill them up, and I bought a can of San Pellegrino lemonade and downed it in one go, dropping the empty can straight into the bin. I headed back to the path ready to tackle the next bit of path - onwards!

After some faffing with directions and a slightly dodgy small section on the main road round a blind corner with no pavement, I headed along the trail above the road, past a hotel, some residential building and then into the car park at Saunton where there was some event going on - security was present and cars were everywhere. It was a bit awkward walking up the road out the car park with big camper vans, caravans and cars squeezing in both directions and me having to balance on a bit of raised grass bank by the side of the road, but I got back onto a quiet woodland path shortly after.

And then I turned onto the golf course. I was a little over 30 miles into the day, a few miles short of the day end target, and the sun was low in the sky at this point. I had a long day planned for tomorrow - 35 miles - and didn't want to stop short of today's planned end point as it would just increase the amount I'd have to walk tomorrow, so I was ignoring some fairly decent looking camping spots around the golf course.

You have to bear in mind, too, that this was my first ever go at wild camping on my own (other than once on Dartmoor, but that doesn't really count as it was in an area you're permitted to camp). Wild camping is not strictly allowed[4], but there's a general principle that if you arrive late, leave early and "leave no trace" then people will usually leave you alone. In the worst case, if asked by someone to leave, then as long as you comply, you're not breaking any law.

Anyway, I wasn't really sure what would be a good spot. Some areas looked physically decent - flat, secluded, that sort of thing - but I could see all sorts of ways that someone could appear out the bushes, drive by, patrol the area etc (bearing in mind I'd not

---

[4] Technically, the offence you're committing is trespass, which is a civil offence. It only becomes a criminal offence if you refuse to move when asked.

long before gone past a warning that I'd entered a military training area and hadn't seen any indication that I'd left it!) and I'd get caught and told to get lost. As much as it wasn't the end of the world, after a long day walking and with another one tomorrow, I *really* didn't want to get told to move on: I wanted a decent night's sleep.

With that in mind, I messaged a friend I haven't spoken to for ages who lives in Braunton - the town I was a few miles from. I knew he had a field that he was using as a camp site and I hoped that it was fairly near and I could have a night somewhere safe and easy, like last night.

He replied, and a few minutes later I was on the phone to Matt. It turns out his campsite was in Woolacombe - 3 hours back from where I was. He had a few suggestions for camp sites and one for a hotel to stay in town, but mentioned that it was all very busy and it was likely I wouldn't be able to find anywhere with space.

By this time, I'd come out the end of the golf course. I had to go on a short detour through some woods due to part of the path being closed off with some kind of staging area for filming of *Aquaman 2*, then came out on the American Road - a concrete and gravel road that ran flat and straight as far as the eye could see.

The sun had set but it was still plenty light enough to walk without a head torch. I was beginning to get concerned about where to stop, and gave The George Hotel in Braunton a call to find out if they had a room - at least then I'd have a solid destination to aim for even if it was a few miles further than I intended to walk. But no, they had nothing.

I phoned Eva (my wife) and explained, asking her to phone around a few campsites and accommodation in town, hoping that she would be able to find somewhere while I carried on walking and keeping an eye out for any decent looking spots.

On the right side of the American Road was a wire fence, and past that fence was Braunton Burrows Site of Special Scientific Interest (SSSI). There were styles at various points along the fence, but I still wasn't sure that it wasn't part of the military training area, and with the burrows being an SSSI I had convinced myself there would be patrols and there was no way I could camp there without quickly being found.

Eventually as I was coming closer to the end of the road, the fence to my right ended and I took that as a sign that this was fair game as an area to camp. I went into a small clearing, but it was full of brambles and uneven ground, and everywhere that looked vaguely reasonable to pitch seemed to be on or right next to a path. Ahead were the back edge of dunes leading towards the sea, and for some reason my brain had marked those as out-of-bounds as they were part of the SSSI, so I didn't even head any further in that direction but returned back to the road. If I'd taken a look at Google Maps, I would have seen that I could have gone a little more towards the coast and found any number of places, but I was starting to panic at this point and clear thinking was going out the window. Eva hadn't called back in a good 20 minutes or so, and that could only mean there wasn't anything available. I was on my own, it was getting dark, I had a big day ahead and I was beginning to lose control.

I gave up on the area on the edge of the Burrows (which on reflection would have been pretty much perfect) and headed back out onto the American Road. Having now put my head torch on, I followed it down to the end, hoping for that magical moment where the perfect spot came into view. There was a car park at Crow Point which initially had some great looking spots behind the bushes, but it didn't take long to spot tissues and condom wrappers everywhere... for some reason that put me off camping there!

By now it was almost completely dark, but I had no other option than to head towards Braunton and try my luck in town. At least there was a supermarket that would still be open for a few more hours and I could get supplies, then figure things out from there.

Walking along the road, I could see marshes to the left bounded by a big, wet ditch on the edge of the road so that side was out. The bank on the right side was raised up a few metres and I climbed up to walk along out of the way of the few cars going to and from the car park. As I looked around, I started thinking that although a bit out in the open, this would do. I could camp here, just over the top of the bank away from the road. No one would come along surely... yeah, this would do! I dumped my bag, started getting the tent out and felt around on the ground to make sure there was nothing sharp or uneven. It was on quite a slant down towards the water, but I'd given up trying for perfection now. But as I went a little further down the hill to check the ground, I realised it was covered in the shells of sea creatures - and with that, the realisation that this was a bank to protect the road from the water which could rise up significantly with the tide, so it would be a *really* bad idea to camp here. With total dejected resignation, I packed the tent back into its bag, slammed it back into my pack, slung that on my back and dropped down to the road level to head into town without any further plan.

I called Chris. We had a chat, he was a few miles back on the golf course and reckoned he could find a spot there where he probably wouldn't be caught, especially if he was packed up before first light. He didn't have any magical suggestions for me other than to keep looking.

I was in despair. I felt totally knackered and overwhelmed with what lay ahead for the next 19 days. It was only the second night and it was all going wrong. Maybe I could walk all night? I had a head torch and experience of night running - in fact, I loved it - so that wasn't a problem. But this wasn't supposed to be a single day ultramarathon - it was days of walking. Multiple days, and I had to think longer than a single day. What would I do tomorrow after no sleep?

In hindsight there's quite a few obvious ways out of this, it wasn't really a cause for panic. But in the dark, after a long day, when tired and inexperienced it all felt like a crushing weight on top of me.

I continued to the first roundabout in town, tipping the distance at just around 37 miles. Ahead was a guy with a pack on his back and a pair of walking poles. My heart lifted - a fellow walker, someone who might be able to help, or at the very least would be in the same situation. I caught up with him, and we had a chat. His name was Bob, and he too couldn't find anywhere, but his plan was just to continue and see how it worked out. He was much more chilled than I was and seemed to be having a great time. I didn't want to tag along on a search for what may only be a decent spot for a single tent which could get awkward, so we said our goodbyes. Standing on one side of the roundabout, with a small gang of teenagers buzzing around on a few mopeds on the other side, I gave Eva a call to see if she had any ideas.

As it turns out, she couldn't find any accommodation, but she had been thinking ahead and found a few spots on the satellite view of Google Maps that looked like good potentials for camping. She's always very good at being realistic in situations, and told me in the nicest way that I had no choice, I was going to have to try somewhere and if I got moved on then just deal with it. I took a quick look on my phone at the spots she'd mentioned and they looked good - finally it felt like there were possibilities. Had I slowed down to just think for a minute rather than panicking, I would probably have done the same thing.

I hung up, headed back up the road away from town and into the darkness. My head torch caught a pair of eyes off the road down a path, and sat there against the bushes was a cat looking at me. I took this as a sign (this is becoming a habit at camp spots!), and headed down the path to take a look, with the cat disappearing as soon as I headed towards it. After 20 or 30 metres, it opened out into a bigger area by what sounded like a weir, it was too dark to tell at this point. There was a flat section of ground just the other side of a raised bank, shielding it from the road. This would do nicely. Nervously, I dumped my bag down on the grass.

The spot was Velator Quay, right next to Knowl Water and just opposite the Home Hardware store. *And* it turns out to be part of the coast path, unlike the road that I'd taken to get into Braunton. Had I gone the right way I may well have spotted this place without all the fuss! The ground was quite long grass, which when folded over under a tent would make a comfortable base.

I switched my head torch to the tiny dim red light so as to be more subtle. With my night vision beginning to come into play, and the late twilight and various lights across the town, there was enough light for me to see what I needed. The sound of water flowing on the weir was comforting and disguised any noise I was making setting up the tent.

It felt like it took forever to get the tent out, lay it in place, put the 5 pegs in, then the walking pole and pull it up to a proper tent shape with the final peg, but once that was done and I could get inside I started feeling a lot better. I didn't bother with the 3 extra guy lines, there wasn't any wind and I wanted to get in as fast as possible. It's funny how a thin sheet of canvas feels like it protects you from the world, hiding you and giving you your own little safe space.

The tent was a bit damp from the previous morning, but I didn't care. It was up, and I was inside. I did the minimal amount of clothes changing as prep for tomorrow as I figured I may get turfed off this spot in the middle of the night and it would be better to get going quickly. I got my sleeping bag out and decided not to bother with the air mat - it would take too long and make too much noise to pump up.

I lay down on the base of the tent and rested the sleeping bag on top of me. After 37 miles of hot walking with a pack on, having been panicking about where to sleep for the last hour or two, it was absolute bliss. It felt heavenly.

For about 10 minutes, anyway.

Then my back made it very clear that it wasn't going to play ball without the air mat. I got the mat out, didn't bother with the inflation bag but lay the whole mat on top of me and spent the next 5 minutes quietly blowing it to size. I then had a right load of hassle trying to get it from on top of me where I'd blown it up, to underneath me where it would serve better as a sleep aid. After much wobbling around and banging into the tent, I finally lay there again, quite a lot more comfortable and ready to sleep. The time was about 10:15pm.

For the first part of the evening, I kept seeing headlights lighting the tent as cars drove down the road. I was sure someone would see me, but I guess I was far enough back or generally inconspicuous enough not to draw much attention. I kept hearing distant voices and was convinced that at any moment I was either going to be kicked out of the area or found by a bunch of drunken youths, but I did get some sleep. I woke up a lot during the night, each time fully awake in an instant when I remembered where I was, then checking my watch. By the time it was 3am, I started to relax, figuring that most people would be in bed and I was unlikely to be disturbed. I fell into a restless sleep until morning.

CHAPTER 5

Day 3: Braunton to Clovelly

Tarmac paths, heat and a fly.

Start Time	**6:42am**
Total Distance	**38.05 miles**
Elevation	**3638 feet**
Total Time	**12 hours 5 mins**
Moving Time	**9 hours 35 mins (15:40 min/mil)**
Steps	**73321**

The alarm went off at 5:40am and woke me from a light sleep. There were the first hints of morning light visible inside the tent.

Knowing where I was and how I probably shouldn't hang around too long into the day was a good incentive to get going quickly. I had no idea what might be outside the tent (ignorance is bliss!), so I thought I'd prepare as much as possible inside, then I could clear everything else up quickly if necessary. I got my gaiters, socks and shoes on (the shorts and t-shirt for today were already on after changing before settling down last night), and unzipped the tent to find out what lurked in the early morning twilight.

It was clear. There was no-one about, and nothing but the sound of water from the weir. Knowing I was already in the process of packing up and moving on I relaxed considerably, a euphoric sense of relief that I'd managed to camp and have at least some sleep in the night after the panic of the previous evening. I munched a few chocolate-covered coffee beans in lieu of a cup of coffee and got going with the packing up.

The grass was wet from dew again - not quite as bad as the previous day but the inside and outside of the tent flysheet was dripping again, probably down to the moisture in the air from the flowing water next to where I had camped. I put the sleeping bag away in its pack and got back into the tent to roll up the inflatable mat so it didn't get wet on the grass. Once that was done, I dragged my little polycro sheet loaded with gear outside from under the tent outer, and started laying various drybags around on the sheet. The tent came down next, 6 pegs and a walking pole out, then a good shake and I squeezed it back in the sack. It didn't feel like it took long, but it was about 45 minutes before I had everything back in the pack ready to go.

My walking poles clip into a pair of special gloves with an attachment loop to clip the pole into between the thumb and index finger. As I put the first glove back on, I felt quite a bit of pain on my hand and on inspection there was a raw patch where it had rubbed the previous day. Better to deal with these things early I thought, so I spent a couple of minutes opening up my pack, getting the first aid kit out, finding a plaster and sticking it to the appropriate place. I then packed everything away.

As I put the second glove on my other hand... I felt quite a bit of pain on my hand where it had rubbed the previous day. Why the hell had I put everything away after the first plaster! Repeating the whole process again, I stuck another plaster to my other hand and checked everything else over before packing back up for the final time. I lifted it onto my back and headed back out onto the road almost exactly 1 hour after my alarm had woken me.

I actually felt good! It was morning, I was ready to go!

Chris sent me a text message saying he had decided that he would head into Braunton from his camp spot on the golf course a few miles back, then get the bus to Bideford (about 16 miles along from where I was) and walk from there. We'd meet up later in the day as we both made our way to the end point of Clovelly, a 35 mile walk for me, but with the first 25 miles pretty much flat.

The Tarka Trail is a 180-mile route inspired by the route travelled by *Tarka the Otter* from Henry Williamson's famous 1927 novel. A fair chunk of it - from Lynton through to Bideford, which included all of yesterday and half of today's walking - is shared with the South West Coast Path. A lot of today took the path of a disused railway so was very flat with a lot of black asphalt. I had to pay attention to cyclists whizzing by - there was a constant flow of people coming towards me on bikes, but you couldn't just step across to avoid them as the chances are there would be someone flying along behind you too - it got quite tiring constantly looking behind and planning which side of the path to be on to improve my chances of making it all the way to Bideford without being mown down by a speeding cyclist.

The route first took me past a military base at Chivenor, alongside the river Taw then over a big bridge into Barnstaple. I had got myself confused between Barnstaple and Bideford, and I thought Chris meant he was getting the bus to the much closer town that I was now just entering the outskirts of. I texted him and said I was heading for the Costa Coffee to get something for breakfast as it was the first place I saw on the map that I was pretty sure would do both food and have a plug to charge my battery.

I detoured off the path heading towards town via a very busy road junction where I had to run across multiple lanes of traffic. I spotted a big Asda supermarket in the distance and sent Chris another message redirecting him there, thinking I could get a breakfast in the cafe. Heading through the car park I was getting a bit annoyed at how far away the entrance was, they're always at the wrong end of the building! I went through the doors and spotted the cafe at the far end of the store. It was closed. Brilliant.

Back out the store, I headed back to the road and texted Chris with a return to the original plan to meet at Costa. It was at this point he texted back saying he was going to *Bideford*, not *Barnstaple*. I quickly checked the map, and realised I was a good few hours behind his target spot. I really am crap at geography!

I went past another roundabout towards Costa and saw it in the distance, the view behind was dominated by the big Tesco supermarket. I was already thinking that Tesco would be a better bet which was confirmed as I passed Costa and found they weren't open until 9am, and even then only for takeaway which wouldn't do me as I was hoping to both sit down and get a spot of juice for my battery.

I went across the large Tesco car park, heading straight for the nice big obvious door right in front of me and into the store, starting to feel very conscious of how long it was taking for me to get breakfast and how far from the coast path I was heading. I asked the security guard by the door about the cafe, and he directed me upstairs. 5 minutes later I sat down with a full English breakfast, some strong black coffee and 2 full water bottles.

I'd spent a little time looking at the map on my phone, and figured out a faster and safer way back to the path which avoided the big dual-carriageway and roundabout that I had crossed on the way here.

After finishing my breakfast, I went into the main store downstairs and picked up a steak slice for later in the day, along with a pack of those chocolate chip brioche buns that are individually wrapped and made with so many chemicals they last until the end of time - perfect!

At just before 9am I'd navigated back through town and was now heading along the Tarka trail on the other side of the river Taw to which I had been walking earlier in the day, on my way to Bideford and starting to slowly bake in the sun. Just before heading off on my adventure, I'd stopped at a friend's shop and bought, amongst other things, a ridiculously expensive hat which held ice (for very hot events) and had a removable, elasticated sun shield that dropped down to protect your neck. I didn't end up bringing the hat, but I did bring the sun shield, so I dug it out of the hip pocket of my pack and twanged it onto the hat I was wearing. It hung down over the back of my neck, and I could immediately feel the heat of the direct sun diminish from my neck. It also made me look absolutely bloody ridiculous, but I didn't care.

After a few miles, I started to get that urge you really hope you don't get when you're walking along a trail that shows no sign of going anywhere near a set of toilets. I checked the OS Map app on my phone and found a couple of places that would potentially have a toilet, judging one to be about 30 minutes away, the other about an hour away, and offered up a prayer to anyone who would listen that I would make it.

I don't remember a huge amount about this section of trail as my mind was otherwise engaged, but I have vague recollections of there being various bridges and railway related furniture, and a tree-covered section so I could take the silly sun shield off my hat. 20 minutes or so later, I came to the disused train station at Fremington and spotted the sign for toilets. I tried the gate - it was locked.

Slightly desperately, I went to the window of the closed cafe. There was a sort-of chain-link shield over the window, but I could hear voices inside, so I called through and asked if there was a toilet nearby. After some considerable hunting for the keys and then finding the right one for the gate, they very kindly opened up the toilet on the platform, and… well, you don't need any more details!

With hands and face washed again (I was taking every opportunity to have a sink wash every time I could), I felt much better setting off again along the path. The cover of the trees had vanished and I was starting to heat up again in the sunshine.

The coast path takes a right turn off the Tarka trail a little after Fremington to take you along a coast section of the Taw rather than plodding along on the tarmac cycleway. The ground got a little sandier and rougher, but the view was a bit more interesting as I went alongside the workings on the edge of the river. Across the water was Chivenor, and just behind there was Velator where I had camped last night. It was less than 2 miles away as the crow flies, but had taken me around 3 and a half hours of walking via Barnstaple to get here. With the route running alongside estuaries and into towns, that was pretty much the theme of the day - taking a very long time to go not very far.

My shorts were really starting to chafe my inner thigh. For the previous two days I'd worn my compression shorts under my running shorts, but in trying to get organised quickly in the tent last night I'd not bothered with the compression shorts. I'd hoped I would get away with it, that maybe I didn't need to be wearing that extra later, but this latest development proved that wasn't the case.

A few miles later, as I entered the car park at Instow I knew it had become critical to sort out the chafing - I was starting to walk in an odd way to avoid the pain of the seams rubbing my legs, and that couldn't go on. I snuck round the back of a small van in the car park, not completely out of view but better than out in the open. I whipped off my running shorts (yes, I still had underwear on!), pulled on my compression shorts and in what was probably the dodgiest moment of the lot, applied a liberal amount of Squirrels Nut Butter anti-chafe stuff by shoving my hands down my shorts! With running shorts back on top, I reappeared from behind the van. I've no idea if anyone saw me and wondered what I was up to, but when you're 3 days into this sort of thing you start to really not care what anyone else thinks. And besides, the chafing was now completely sorted, no pain at all. I had confirmed that I should *definitely* be wearing those compression shorts. The same couldn't be said for the sore on my back - it let itself be known as I dropped the pack back on my back, and as it was fairly handy, I stuck another load of Squirrels Nut Butter on that area to try and reduce the rubbing.

I checked my phone, and noticed that Chris had sent a message letting me know he'd had food in a Wetherspoons in Bideford, and was ready to head off towards Clovelly. This was great news - not so much that Chris was heading off, but more knowing that there was a pub in town where I could get food, water and coffee and set on my way with a decent lunch.

This boosted me up mentally, and I continued on the long plod from Instow to Bideford, with the big Torridge bridge seemingly ever-present in the distance. At Instow, the river Taw flows out into the sea and south of the village is the river Torridge which I was now walking beside. Sometime after Instow, I passed under the Torridge bridge and was on the home straight into Bideford. As I reached East-the-Water, I found the old station and the Bideford Railway Heritage Centre, consisting of a museum in a train carriage at the station, and a restaurant in the next carriage. There was also a large gathering of bikes to avoid, and I came off the path here, down a slope and onto the road over Old Bideford Bridge into town.

Back in the traffic again, I had to cross a couple of busy roads which felt a bit surreal after a few days without meeting much traffic, and I had to concentrate to make sure I wasn't going to get run over. Once over the road, I checked Google Maps on my phone, walked a bit further, checked the phone again, turned up the next road and then into the Rose Salterne pub at just after

11:30am. Bob, the guy from Braunton that I saw late the previous night, was just leaving the pub at the same time I was entering and yelled across, but I completely missed him - I was completely focused on my mission to sit down and eat!

Not wanting to further ruin an already pretty ropey Wetherspoons seat, I whipped out my ever-useful polycro sheet from the bottom of my bag to sit on. Under the seats there were plugs, so I took the opportunity to charge my phone and battery. I was a little too late for breakfast, but again, faced with a menu choice including my usual favourite "naughty food" of chips and burgers I opted for a jacket potato. And a pint of Guinness... I heard it was good for you.

Refreshed after my meal, I headed off from the pub at a little after midday. Having crossed the bridge in Bideford earlier, I was now on the western side of the Torridge, heading North towards Appledore, after which I'd go around the Northam Burrows peninsula and down the coast to Westward Ho!

Still flat along the river Torridge, on the ground I noticed occasional footprint markers which I didn't realise until sometime later were indicating the direction of the coast path. After passing the boats on the quayside the path changed from tarmac cycleway to riverside woodland path once out of the town. I made a brief mistake somewhere around the Torridge Bridge where I thought I had to go down to the water across some particularly sticky mud, but luckily it turned out to be a different route inland otherwise I probably would have ended up losing a shoe! The path undulated and passed in and out of the woods, and after crossing a road and heading down another section of path I saw a walker in the distance. As I approached, he turned and said hello - it was Bob! We had a brief chat; it turns out last night he'd walked further along the Tarka trail and found a spot by the side of the river and was making good progress today. He also mentioned seeing me go into the Wetherspoons in Bideford as he was coming out and shouting over to me, but that I didn't respond. If memory serves correctly, his target for the day was Westward Ho! We wished each other well and I carried on[5].

I must admit to being a bit bored of the lack of *coast* on the coast path at this point. I'd been going for approaching 6 hours now on a mostly flat, urban trail, and although I was now in woods it didn't feel like the coast path I knew and loved. We were close to towns, and it really felt like it. I was longing to get back to the sea, to the rocks, to the hills and rough terrain, although I was doing my best to try and appreciate the lack of hills in this section and the speed I could move at.

Coming into Appledore was like a breath of fresh air. The path wound along the quay at the edge of the river, with a wonderful view of boats and water across to Instow where I'd been 2 and a half hours previously. I spotted those metal footprints on the ground again, and figured it must just be some

---

[5] I mentioned the SWCP Facebook group to Bob, and he joined up a day or two later. He finished the whole path on 17th October in 45 days – well done Bob!

local tradition. My internal guidance system had another strong desire to explore a car park, and after a fight with my GPS I found the right route out, again noticing the footprints on the ground… that was when it dawned on me that they were coast path markers! I followed the path along quaint, narrow residential roads with multicoloured houses, now happy I was going the right way after spotting a few sets of footprints on the pavement, and then around the top of the village, headed into the Northam Burrows Country Park.

The sun was still blazing down, but the wind was picking up on this tip of land between the rivers and the sea. I walked along the flat road, beginning to get a little fed up with the direct sun. I retrieved the elasticated sunshield from my hip pocket and twanged it over my cap, but the wind was strong and gusty and kept nearly blowing it from my head so I had to take it off. I fiddled around behind my head in the pocket on the top of my bag, dragging out my "essentials" plastic bag. In there was my SPF 50 sunblock for babies, in theory as hypoallergenic as possible. I slapped a load over my neck and arms, packed the tube away in the bag and put it all back into my pack, all without stopping.

This was becoming a mentally tough day, and it was beginning to turn into a baking hot one as well. I was beginning to get a bit concerned about getting water along the route. The walking was still good - I was happily walking miles in around 15 minutes, sometimes faster - but what felt like a pointless excursion of a few miles around a headland was messing with my tired brain.

The fact that the whole of the South West Coast Path is basically a bunch of "pointless diversions around headlands" - and that I loved that about it - didn't really factor into my thinking at that point. And my hat kept nearly getting blown off in the increasing wind, which was really starting to piss me off!

After walking for what felt like too long through an area with cars dotted around beside the road - and despite looking like the perfect area, not a single ice cream van - I got to the top of the park and started heading along Greysands Beach. Out of nowhere came a golf course. The path alongside the course was sandy and undulating, like walking on heathland, and my feet kept slipping sideways in the sand, slowing my pace. In the distance I could see a building and I was really hoping it was a cafe so I could sort my water situation out, but first I had to get round this golf course.

Through the car park and into the cafe (it was!), I got 2 cans of drink and filled my water bottles again with water. I stuck one can in the side of my bag alongside a water bottle (it turns out I could fit two bottles/cans on each side which was handy) and drank the other in one go. Then I carried on into Westward Ho!

Westward Ho! is noted for its irritation caused to people with auto-correcting document editors, caused by the exclamation mark at the end of its name. It's not me being dramatic - the name is actually Westward Ho!, rather than Westward Ho. The name comes from the Charles Kingsley novel of 1855 of the same name (including the exclamation mark), which became a bestseller and hence entrepreneurs saw an opportunity to cash in by boosting tourism in the area. It's the only place in the UK with an exclamation mark in the name, and one of only 2 in the world (the other is Saint-Louis-du-Ha! Ha! in Quebec, Canada, which boasts not one but two of the little blighters).

Now I'm sure it's a lovely place, but in my state of mind at that point I really disliked it. It was full of people, and full of traffic. The narrow pavement into town was awkward as nobody was considering anyone else. The whole place just felt full of tourists on their own holiday with no care in the world for anyone outside their personal group. The caravan parks, noisy arcades, and packed beach areas were the antithesis of my feelings about the coast path. After the year we've had with very little tourism, it's good that businesses are getting back on their feet, but I just didn't like the whole atmosphere of the place.

I headed through the town without slowing down. The one thing I did notice and like was the sea pool, built into the rocks, near the far end of town. It was built by the Victorians back in Victorian times (funny, that) but damaged significantly in the early 2000's. Repairs and renovations were completed in 2016 and the sea pool is now back to its former glory, looking rather magnificent with the rocks and sea as a backdrop.

Just past the sea pool, I stopped at a toilet block at the end of town. After peeing something similar to the colour of strong tea, it was a good reminder that today was a hot day and I wasn't drinking enough so I had the can of Diet Coke that was tucked in my bag straight away and headed on up to the path out of Westward Ho!

It was just after 2:30pm, I was 25 miles into the day and I'd hardly climbed any hills at all. That was about to change in the last 11 miles.

I was back in my element. Just around the corner from Westward Ho! the path turned back into the trail again, running alongside the sea, through fields, and up and down hills with views to take your breath away. The coast headed south away from me and in the distance I could see it curve round to the west on the Hartland peninsula, with Clovelly - my destination - clearly visible, its white buildings hanging to the steep coastal hills in the far away.

The only issue was the incessant sun. And this was causing me to get through water at a rate of knots. Within a few miles of leaving the town I'd drained my first water bottle, leaving me with 850ml of water left and potentially 4 hours of walking remaining. I had my water filter with me to enable me to clean up water from streams but this sort of terrain didn't really have much access to any water sources, although I kept looking. On a few occasions I could *hear* water, but each time I couldn't actually get to it.

I kept going. Up and down some fairly big hills, then down one huge hill and steps to a beach, only to immediately come back up the other side. Typical coast path - but even with the sun sapping my energy I knew this was what I loved about it, and I was actually happy to be going down and up rather than being on a flat, tarmac cycle path.

I chatted with someone just out for a short walk and asked about a shop or somewhere to get water, but they'd come from Peppercombe cottages just around the corner and they didn't know the area well. A little further along I found the first piece of shade in over an hour, and realised how hungry I felt. I got the peppered steak slice I'd bought from Tesco earlier that morning out of my pack, and considered whether having sat in the warm top of my pack for the best part of 8 hours it would still be safe to eat. I dabbled with a bit of Salmonella poisoning about 20 years ago, and really didn't want to shit myself all the way to Land's End because of a dodgy snack. But I was hungry now, and I just went for it and took the first bite. It tasted absolutely delicious - warmed by the sun, it was like it had just come out of a microwave at the perfect temperature (which, I hear, is exactly the way they heat Ginster's products in *Michelin* star establishments) and I wolfed the remains down. 20 minutes later, I felt a whole lot better, a good reminder of just how much of an impact not keeping on top of food can have on both your physical and mental state.

The problem with eating, though, is that it accentuates thirst, and with limited water this was a problem. At the bottom of the next hill, I rounded a corner to see a building - Peppercombe Coach House, now a rest stop for walkers. It's *bound* to have a tap, I thought to myself, and headed inside. There was no tap.

Back outside on the narrow stone road, I met a couple in a Mercedes. They were looking for somewhere I didn't know how to get to, and after passing on this information they then proceeded to nearly run me over as I continued on the path. I'm about 80% sure it was accidental.

Up and down a few more hills, I found a sign to Buck's Mills a few miles away, and hoped that there I would finally find somewhere to get water as I was now getting really quite low. Just before Buck's Mills, I talked to a couple who told me about another walker about 30 minutes ahead of me and described Chris pretty well… I was catching him up!

It hadn't been the intention to have a race, but it now turned into one, and gave me something to focus on. I knew Chris was a fair distance ahead, but I was gaining on him and with a few more hours to go I could catch up with him. Off I went with a newfound purpose and energy.

Water was still an issue though, I was half way through my second bottle, down to around 400ml, and rationing as much as I could in the heat. I went down the steps and steep hill into Buck's Mills and I could hear running water. Excellent - I could use my filter and get some water for my bottles now. I got down into the village but there was no obvious source of the water. No matter, it had to be round here somewhere. I asked a couple who weren't local, but they sent me up the path to a house where some local people lived and were doing things in the garden outside the house.

I had a chat with the house owner who kindly offered me the remainder of his water "from the spring" (which I took to mean the fresh, clean, clear water that I could hear running through the village) to top up my bottle. It was only half of one of my bottles, but I figured Clovelly was only a few miles away and it would do now that things were cooler under the shade of the trees. We got chatting about some running in the area, and he explained that in a couple of miles and not too many hills the path opened out into the Hobby Drive, an old horse way which was flatter and led all the way into Clovelly. We spent so long chatting about running on various parts of the route he even offered me a cup of tea. Remembering that Chris was getting away from me as I stood still, I declined, but thanked him for the water and got off up the hill out of Buck's Mills.

That hill went on forever! Every time I thought I was near the top, it turned out to be a false summit and there was more to climb. It wasn't particularly steep after the first section, but it was enough to know you were going uphill, with a few cheeky steep bits thrown in for good measure. Under the cover of trees, the heat of the sun was lessened and with the water top-up I was drinking regularly to try and replenish some lost fluids. The spring water from Buck's Mills tasted a bit odd, but I figured it was just because it wasn't tap water. I went through gates and round the edges of fields, and was beginning to wonder if the Hobby Drive would ever appear, this tantalising promise of flatter ground and a more pleasant entry into Clovelly.

The South West Coast Path marker signs were messing with me too - the distances on them suggested I had further to go than I'd originally thought, and to start with I'd ignored them and assumed they were wrong (not a bad assumption as there are many stories of the SWCP marker signs having incorrect distances). But as more and more of them confirmed the distances I had to give in to the idea that it was probably another 1-2 miles further than I'd thought it was going to be. The track on my GPS ended a little before Clovelly, so my distance target for the day was short of the actual end point, but I had assumed it was only a few hundred metres rather than a mile or two which feels quite significant at the end of a long day.

Finally, at 6 o'clock and 34 miles into the day, I hit the fabled Hobby Drive. It *was* like a road. It was wide, and the path was smooth enough for a horse drawn carriage to travel along. But it wasn't flat by any stretch of the imagination. It was up initially, then quite a lot of downhill, and all on hard packed gravel with sharp stones sticking out, which isn't brilliant when you're wearing fairly minimally cushioned trail running shoes.

I swigged more water, noticing the odd taste… kind of like gone-off milk. And at that point I noticed the dead fly in my bottle. Oh, great. Maybe this was less "spring" water and more "marsh" water. After my potentially dodgy warm steak slice, now I was drinking water with dead insects in. If I didn't get ill, I would be lucky!

If I hadn't already walked more than 35 miles, I think I would have really enjoyed the Drive. It wound around in word, with steep sides covered in ferns and trees. Occasional quaint little bridges guided it over the fast-flowing water that ran down the valleys. And there were *loads* of pheasants - every minute or two there would be a few running around in the path the way pheasants do – in all directions at once, looking like a panicking cartoon bird trying to escape a hunter! Then as I vaguely approached them, there would be a great clatter and flapping of wings as Mr Pheasant and all his local mates hiding in the bushes tried to get airborne.

But today I *had* walked more than 35 miles, and I was knackered. I knew I was near the end so I was trying to walk quickly, but my heels were getting pretty painful with the constant striking of the hard packed ground. I kept changing the music on my MP3 player - *Muse, Foo Fighters, Architects* - hoping for something that would boost me through to the end, but nothing was working at this point.

In the distance, a couple with a pair of dogs were up to something in the bushes and as I passed, they were busy rearranging their considerable packs. "Are you meeting your mate in Clovelly?" they asked. It turns out Chris was no more than a few minutes ahead… *that* was the thing I needed to sort me out: the race was on!

I went off like a bat out of hell, doing 14-minute mile pace along the path and at 6:45pm and just over 36½ miles after putting away my tent in Braunton that morning I popped out of the trees at Mount Pleasant, the top of Clovelly. I spent a couple of minutes trying to call Chris, but there was no connection to his phone. I figured the pub would be a better place to contact him from (obviously!), so headed down the very steep cobblestone path into Clovelly, finding out pretty quickly that this sort of ground was no good for walking poles. As I turned the corner, I saw Chris coming out of the New Inn with a pint and menu in hand! He'd pipped me by *2 minutes...* that was a close one!

Chris had got the bus to Bideford, had some food and then headed off to Appledore. From there, he'd cut across to Westward Ho! missing out the Northam Burrows section, and headed off from there a few hours ahead of me.

There was a set of tables on a flat section overlooking the famous steep, cobbled street of Clovelly, directly opposite the New Inn. Behind us, a couple arrived with huge packs and a couple of dogs - it was the two I'd seen a mile or so before Clovelly, who told me about Chris being a few minutes ahead. They were Tab and Zo, and were doing Combe Martin to Bude with their two dogs and huge 18kg packs full of camping gear and dog food!

Chris and I both had a nice Goan curry with rice and poppadoms. It was tasty but not massive - a sensible portion for anyone who hadn't just walked the best part of 40 miles. We topped up with a couple of pints of local tipple and a pudding each.

Tab and Zo very sensibly booked themselves into the hostel that we were actually sitting outside of, and we said goodbye to them as the sun disappeared. I'd heard from the "fly" guy I chatted to in Buck's Mills that there were plenty of camping opportunities past Clovelly, just a little way further along the path.

It was now dark, and with our head torches on we headed up the cobbles and back onto the coast path out of the village in the direction of Hartland. After half a mile or so, we'd found a few potential spots, dismissed most of them for various reasons and headed back to the most promising site in a large grassy field. We were both really tired after the long, hot day, and just got on with setting up tents at a little before 10pm. There was a light on the far side of the area, but being just a single white light, we couldn't tell what it was or how far away. To be honest, by that point I didn't care, I just wanted to get in the tent and get a good night's sleep.

Although not really uncomfortable, I couldn't get to sleep. I could hear the tree above me creaking in the wind. It was an old oak tree, and I couldn't be sure that the sound coming from it wasn't a big branch about to snap and land on top of me. I kept thinking of the term *dead man's pitch* - the term for when you set your tent up under an old tree - and that wasn't making me feel any better. I tried to dismiss the thoughts, but they sat there in my mind until eventually at around midnight the wind blew enough that one of my tent pegs popped out. I went outside to sort it, and walked around the tree, climbing a little and pulling various branches. At the back of the tree, I saw two significant lumps of branches on the ground that I judged had fallen within the last month or two and decided that was it - I was moving!

So out came 9 tent pegs, and I dragged the tent 10 metres into the middle of the field. It wasn't too bad to move actually, I had expected everything to collapse and be a nightmare to set back up, but when I quickly got the pegs back in the tent was actually set up better than I had it originally. The only issue was that I'd moved from a flat bit of ground to a sloping section, but at least I wasn't going to die under a tree now!

I lay there, comfortable but awake. 1 o'clock. 2 o'clock. 3 o'clock. Still awake. Why couldn't I sleep? I was thinking too much. I was beginning to lose it again mentally. There was too much to do without enough sleep. Why was it so difficult to just *sleep*?

At just before 4am, I did something I almost never do. I got my phone out and wrote a vaguely emotional Facebook post:

"Beautiful views and brutal sun - this was the bit between Westward Ho! and Clovelly.

I'm writing this in a tent. I haven't slept so far and it's 0350 now. Current plan is to get a bus to Bude and prop up a bar until the (booked) campsite is available, have a shower and consider.

I can walk the miles - in fact I am really surprised at how relatively easy I can handle that bit. I can put up with aches and pains - shredded back from the bag, rubbed hips, blisters under calluses on my feet etc.

But an hour either side of 12+ hour days setting up and putting down camping stuff, not knowing where/if I can stop, only a few hours sleep in 3 days… it's messing with my head and I'm losing it a bit now.

I want to can it now, but 4am isn't a good time to make decisions. A day off seems like a compromise.

Will update soon…"

I'm not quite sure what I was hoping to achieve, I just felt like I needed to get my feelings off my chest and maybe someone could reply back with a gem, a comment that would sort the problem out, maybe put things in perspective. Whatever the result, I needed a break.

With my phone still out, I checked bus times and found one early in the morning to Bude, and that was now my plan, I was taking the next day off. I wouldn't be walking to Bude. I'd skip that bit, take a rest day and hope I could manage the remainder of my adventure.

After about another hour, I finally fell asleep.

CHAPTER 6
Day 4: Going Nowhere

Six pints and a bloke called Dave.

Start Time	**7am-ish**
Total Distance	**A few miles**
Elevation	**A few feet**
Total Time	**A few hours**
Moving Time	**A few hours**
Steps	**11181**

What felt like a few moments later, it was 5:50am and my watch was buzzing away. I'd had about an hour of sleep, but I was feeling fairly happy with my new plan. Today was about mental recovery, not walking, and that would set me up for the rest of my adventure.

It wasn't what I'd planned, but I couldn't figure out a way to get my head in the right place to walk today's section. I was supposed to be walking from Clovelly to Bude, 28 miles with 8,000ft of climb and the second half (from Hartland to Bude) generally being described as one of the toughest sections of the whole coast path. That didn't put me off - I was genuinely looking forward to this section, especially as I'd run about half of the toughest bit a month earlier - but I couldn't face it with an overwhelming mental tiredness.

Since my post on Facebook in the middle of the night I'd received a bunch of replies to my message. The general consensus was that I was doing too much, and taking a break wasn't a bad thing. A couple of messages stood out to me. Howard, who I hadn't seen for over 5 years and lives in Newquay sent:

"Keep going, you can do it...I'm coming to meet you Saturday morning."

And Pat, who I respect hugely for not only being a genuinely nice bloke but also a GB ultrarunner and winner of many very, very long races sent a message on WhatsApp:

"Months in the planning Rich....
Do not pull the plug on it. You knew before you started it wasn't going to be easy.
3 big days in some serious heat. You must be a fair bit ahead of schedule.....
Have a couple of easier days.
Feel free to bounce shit off me pal.
Enjoy it"

With the promise of an easier rest day, and the dawn light building, which always boosts my spirits, I felt... ok. I wasn't delighted, but I would see how things panned out over the day. I now had no intention of quitting here, I'd take the rest day and continue on tomorrow, hopefully with all the problems in my head sorted.

I told Chris my plan, and he was happy to take an easy day as well. We packed up at a leisurely pace, enjoying packing away tents that were completely dry for the first morning so far. Presumably there wasn't a lot of moisture in the air at Clovelly. As the morning brightened, it became clear that although we were in a field with trees around the edge, the light we saw last night while setting up the tents was a house on the other side of the fence, not too far from us. We may have been fairly lucky not getting caught there!

All packed up, we headed back up to the visitor centre to wait for the bus. As we walked along the path, glimpses through the trees showed an amazing sunrise and when we got out into the open at Mount Pleasant, we both spent a couple of minutes just watching the beautiful golden light show and snapping a few phone photos.

The timetable was a bit confusing with various shaped markers dotted around representing modifications for different times of the year - with our fuddled brains it was difficult to know whether the bus that may or may not turn up would be for school kids only, or whether it was a public service. We both got phones out to look at the various bus times apps we had. With almost no signal, it was the usual click, wait, refresh, go back, hold the phone above your head, do the magic phone-signal dance, walk around the building and eventually get told the page won't load. But we did, in the end, find that we could get a definite public bus to Bideford a few minutes after the Bude bus may-or-may-not turn up. And we knew there was a pub in Bideford where we could get breakfast, coffee and charge batteries. We had a plan!

The Bude bus turned up early. It was empty, and it *was* a public service so we could have got on it. But after it waited for a few minutes and then headed off promptly at 7:35am, we sat slightly nervously waiting for the next bus to turn up. The bus gods were looking down on us and it did indeed turn up at the expected time. By 8am we were well and truly on our way in the opposite direction we should have been going: back to Bideford.

Each day walking, I calculated I was burning 4-5,000 calories. Add on the 2,000 or so you need to just be alive, and I should have been eating 6-7,000 calories a day to fully replenish. Which was an absolute impossibility. In reality you don't need all of that when moving at a slower pace as part of the energy requirement will be met by burning body fat, but at best I was getting maybe 3,000 calories a day, leaving a gap of a good few thousand calories. By this fourth day I was not only tired from lack of sleep, but also from a fairly significant calorie deficit.

Back in Bideford, I tucked into my first breakfast of the day - a Wetherspoons Big Breakfast, along with a never-ending cup of coffee. We stayed in the pub, chatting for quite a few hours, during which time I also wrote a set of notes on my phone about the previous days so I wouldn't forget what we'd been up to. I ordered a breakfast wrap (very nice!) and started on the Guinness too - as I said before, it's good for you. They wouldn't lie, would they?

While sat in the pub we were both checking our phones to find the bus times from Bideford to Bude. It was ridiculous. There were 2 busses a day, otherwise you had to go via Okehampton or Hartland, doubling the journey time and requiring a change. Having said that, we weren't in a particular rush, but we had a campsite booked in Bude and it would be nice to get all set up in the light and get a good night's sleep. So, a bit after 1pm we headed out to the bus stop to get on our way to Bude via Hartland.

Of slight concern with this journey was that we had about 50 minutes on the bus, then only 5 minutes before the next bus left. I was aware that it would be pretty easy to lose 5 minutes on a 50 minutes bus journey and miss the connection, but hoped that it would be OK. Otherwise, it was about a 90-minute wait for the next one in what looked like a pretty quiet village.

Part way on the journey out of Bideford, a guy who was obviously a walker with a pack on his back got on and spent a good few minutes talking to the driver about his onward journey, trying to figure out the details of getting all the way to Tintagel. I was looking at my watch, thinking we were starting to get a bit tight for time now. We got going again eventually and headed on to Hartland.

There are not many things a West Country bus driver will give way to while thundering down narrow country lanes, but a bloody great tractor with a huge trailer appears to be one of them. Close to our destination we lost another few minutes as our bus reversed back to let one pass, and as we approached our connecting stop, we had the pleasure of watching the other bus drive away in the opposite direction. An hour and a half to kill… first thought: where's the pub?

The guy who spent the time talking to the bus driver earlier in the journey had also got off here, having just missed the same connection as us. His name was Dave, and we got chatting and all headed off to the pub across the road - the Hart Inn.

It was closed.

So we walked to the next one - the Kings Arms.

That was closed too.

It was starting to feel as if we were acting out Michael Rosen's new book *We're Going on a Pub Hunt*. "We can't go over it, we can't go under it… we'll have to try the one down the road."

Further along the street was a shop, and intelligence gathered here suggested the Anchor down the road may be open. Off we went as it started to rain a little, finding the Anchor and it's wonderful, inviting and most importantly *unlocked* door. We went inside and managed to get lost in the shop area… A pub with a shop? Slightly quirky, but this was Devon after all. We made our way to a seat by the window, dumped bags and headed off to the bar.

With round 1 ordered, we sat down and had a great chat. It turns out Dave had been a teacher for 12 years but was changing careers to go back to engineering where he had started. Chris and I met at university doing electronic engineering, but during the course I headed towards the software side of things, while Chris continues on to be an expert in electronics. Around the table we had a fair chunk of the engineering disciplines - between us we were qualified to solve almost any problem both late and over-budget. With another pint each, we chatted about various companies we'd worked for, where we lived, and what our plans were. The alcohol was waking me up, but sending Chris to sleep as he seemed to be staring at the wall and almost nodding off to sleep. Soon, it was time to head back up the road, past the shop, the King's Arms and the Hart Inn to get the last bus of the day, so we'd better not miss this one!

The bus journey to Bude was uneventful. I spent time chatting to Dave while Chris dozed on a seat opposite, and during quiet times I stared out the window and was actually getting excited about walking again tomorrow. The day off had been much needed - it had refreshed me, and now I was ready to get going again.

Sometime after 5pm, Chris and I said goodbye to Dave who had found a way to finish off his original journey to the accommodation he had booked in Tintagel. He was walking back towards Bude tomorrow and I was heading out from there, so we agreed to keep an eye out for each other along the route.

Chris and I crossed the road and headed into the Globe pub for dinner. Another pint and a fairly mediocre lasagne landed on the table. While we ate, the rain came down. An absolute torrent, with rivers running in the gutter of the road against the curb. Just as I was starting to imagine pitching the tent in a deluge, it stopped and brightened up. The timing could not have been more perfect!

We headed towards the campsite via the Co-op shop where I got some mini pork pies and liquorice allsorts to tide me over for the next few days. It's difficult to make sensible decisions on what food you need for the next 24 hours or so when you've just eaten dinner and are absolutely knackered… I should have got more really, to make sure I wouldn't go short on nutrition. But at least my brain was half working - with yesterday being so hot, I got a bottle of Lucozade drink that I could keep in my pack for emergencies, taking my total water carrying capacity to 2.2 litres.

I would rather carry a little extra weight and have enough fluid to last if the weather was hot again.

Chris's boots were old and not in a brilliant state at the start of the walk, and during our first few days the outer material had split around the heel. Being a practical engineering sort, he got a pot of superglue from the shop so that he could do a makeshift repair that would hopefully last through to the point where he would have to head home in a few days.

The campsite was a bit further away than we both thought, and up more of a hill than we would have liked, but on the plus side it was in the direction of our travel the next day, so effectively we were cutting a mile or so off tomorrow's plan by walking it today.

We arrived, phoned through and sorted the details. Eva had booked the site, but as it was all Covid'y at the time we weren't met by anyone, just told over the phone to pick a spot and that there were showers and toilets in the buildings at the bottom of the slope, which was all we needed. We picked a flat spot near the hedge at the top of the site, and for the first time on this trip we set our tents up slowly, carefully… and in daylight.

Once our luxury accommodation was erected, the showers beckoned. I walked down to the wooden building at the bottom of the field hidden in trees, not quite sure what to expect. Through the door, there was a shower cubicle. Now these were bog standard shower cubicles, fed by some kind of eco solar system, but that shower was one of the best experiences of my life! If you take away creature comforts for a few days, the little things - like a hot shower - mean so much. I was clean again!

At this point my super lightweight microfibre towel which was about the size of a standard piece of paper seemed like a bad idea. Like a chamois though, if you worked in sections - dry one arm, wring out the towel, dry the other arm, wring out the towel - then you could get somewhere approaching dryness. I still had to put on some smelly worn clothes and I wasn't exactly bone dry as I tried to pull on my unworn running leggings for the night, but at least my skin wasn't all sweaty and dirty and I felt a lot better for it.

It was quite a bit darker when I came out of the shower, and walking back up the field I passed some benches near our tent with one person sitting on them. It looked like they were looking at me. As I got closer, my appalling vision helped me out enough for me to recognise Chris, so I took a seat. After his shower, he'd taken the opportunity to empty a pot of superglue into the various cracks and splits on his boots and was waiting for them to dry. We didn't talk much, both of us were absolutely knackered, but we did enjoy the view down the hill, with the big dishes of GCHQ Bude in the distance and the mist beginning to form now the sun had disappeared below the horizon.

Not much past 8pm, we were in our tents. With batteries charged from our morning in the pub, I treated myself to a podcast - I'd been trying not to use my phone much up to now as I was conserving batteries which had meant only music from my little old MP3 player and nothing current.

115

I stuck on a BBC podcast about maths with Hannah Fry[6], and she mentioned a quote that really struck a chord with me:

"I'm describing the glory, and the glory feels very sweet because there's *so much pain*! … the key difference between people who are mathematicians and not mathematicians – it isn't that mathematicians find it easy, it's that mathematicians *enjoy how hard it is*"

Swap *mathematician* for *runner*, and it seemed to explain a lot about why I like doing silly things like trying to complete the coast path. It's not about finding it easy… it's about enjoying the suffering and relishing in the aftermath!

A few minutes later I fell asleep and had what was almost certainly the best night sleep I've ever had in a tent.

---

[6] "The Life Scientific" with Hannah Fry, released on 7th September 2021 and available on the BBC iPlayer app if you hunt around (at least at the time of writing)

CHAPTER 7

Day 5: Bude to Port Isaac

Flying to King Arthur, grumbling with Doc Martin.

Start Time	**7:04am**
Total Distance	**30.61 miles**
Elevation	**7694 feet**
Total Time	**10 hours 26 minutes**
Moving Time	**8 hours (16:06mins/mile)**
Steps	**60016**

The light patter of rain on my tent woke me before my alarm at a few minutes before 6am. I'd noticed some fairly heavy rain in the night, but slept so well that I was only awake momentarily, just enough to hear it hammering on the flysheet. The tent held up very well, no wet spots inside and no more water inside the tent than the normal amount that seemed to gather as condensation from me breathing in the night.

I checked the DarkSky app on my phone which told me what to expect on the rain front for the next hour, and it looked like the rain was subsiding soon. I called over to Chris in a voice that was balanced between getting his attention in the tent next door, and not waking the whole campsite at 6am. He was awake, and I let him know it might be worth waiting for a couple of minutes for the rain to stop. It didn't stop completely, but rain sounds much louder inside the tent anyway and once the door was open I found it was only lightly spitting.

I did the usual pack up of mat and sleeping bag inside the tent so as not to soak it on wet ground. With everything out the way, you can lay the mat out flat on the floor of the tent, and then fold along the creases into a fairly narrow strip. Starting at the opposite end to the valve, you quickly roll the mat up, with it getting increasingly fatter and wider until you give up, unroll it and carefully, inch by inch, roll, tuck, swear at and shove the mat into shape. Eventually you end up with something that doesn't look like it will quite fit into the pouch, but always seems to. The sleeping bag is easier - you take a massive, puffed-up sleeping bag, and stuff it into a tiny sack. Keep pushing, pushing and pushing some more as it sucks your hand into the ball of compressed feathers, extract said hand and then pretty much sit on the sack and clip it closed. Job done.

The rain was very light now, and with my collection of bits and bobs on the polycro sheet outside, I demolished the tent, shook off the water, squeezed it into the sack and then put that into the plastic bag to keep everything else dry. I took the opportunity to munch the two mini pork pies I'd bought at the Co-op the previous evening as my breakfast, and jolly nice they were too.

I shoved most of the rest haphazardly into my pack, keeping out the drybag with my wash gear in, and headed down to the wooden wash block to perform my ablutions. I filled up water bottles and re-packed the remainder of my stuff into my pack properly while still under the cover of the wash block, out of the rain which had started up again a little heavier. We left the site just after 7am and walked down the road towards Upton at the north end of Widemouth Bay where we met the coast path.

Today's plan was that I would walk to the end point about a mile short of Port Isaac. According to the calculations on The Plan this was 26 miles from our start point on the path. Chris, meanwhile, would walk at a more leisurely pace to Boscastle which was around the 15-mile mark, and then catch a couple of busses (probably via Dubai and Australia knowing Cornish busses) to Port Isaac then walk up the hill to where I would be basking in the glory of having found the world's best camping spot. It all sounded totally feasible and moderately sensible.

Once we got on the coast path, we said our goodbyes for the day and I picked up the pace and headed off. It was one of those rare times I headed in the right direction. To be honest, it would have been pretty difficult to go in the wrong direction as it was either west (very wet), north (wrong) or south (right). But I did manage to make 3 small mistakes in the first 3 miles, so everything was functioning perfectly normally with my sense of direction.

Mentally I felt OK and was happy to be back on the path, even on this dull day that threatened significant amounts of rain. My legs and body certainly felt good after the day off yesterday. The sore patch on my back had begun to toughen and heal, without having a pack rubbing it all day, and I didn't notice any pain or discomfort as I walked out of Widemouth. My head was taking a while to get into the game though - I hadn't really woken up, and I was struggling to get my brain to maintain the pace my legs seemed happy to do. The weather wasn't helping, it couldn't quite decide whether to rain or not so it was just damp in the air. It was warm too, so there was no point putting my coat on as I'd just boil.

Somewhere around St Gennys, about a mile or so from Crackington Haven, I met a guy who was walking the whole of the Cornish Coast Path. He'd started in Plymouth at the Devon/Cornwall border and was nearing the end which was about 6 miles north of Bude at Morwenstow, a point I should have passed yesterday had I not been slacking in a pub. He mentioned that there was a cafe at Crackington Haven which boosted my spirits as I hadn't looked at potential stops and had it in my head that the first refreshments would be around Boscastle - now I knew that I should be able to get some breakfast soon.

About 15 minutes later I dropped down into Crackington Haven and stopped at the Cabin Cafe. With a can of coke in hand and a Farmer's Breakfast and americano ordered I sat down in a chair and tried not to make too much of a mess on the floor from my muddy poles and shoes. The coffee came quickly and shortly afterwards the biggest breakfast I think I've ever had - I must have looked hungry! Seconds later, a lady came half-running out of the kitchen to load the forgotten sausages onto my plate, making it even bigger. Toast, bacon, eggs, mushrooms, little new potatoes, beans and now sausages… I spent 20 minutes trying to eat it all up but had to leave some in the end. I was full to bursting and also a bit concerned about what it was going to feel like getting back into a decent walking pace.

I needn't have worried. Leaving exactly half an hour after I arrived, I headed out and up the hill towards Boscastle, feeling good - awake from the coffee, fully satiated from the food but not uncomfortably full. Ahead there was a man walking slowly up the big hill, a huge pack on his back and poles in hand. He was called Stefan and was in his 60's, out walking a section of the coast path over a few days. We spoke a bit and he told me about his training, walking with the pack up Box Hill near where he lived. He kept telling me that I was wonderful for doing the path at the speed I was going, but I was far more impressed with a guy in his 60s that didn't look super fit sticking on that massive pack and getting on with walking a good chunk of miles on tough terrain. What an inspiration! I hope I can still do things like that in 20 years time.

The terrain went up and down, the sky stayed grey and foreboding but luckily hadn't delivered much of the rain in the clouds to where I was walking. A little after midday, pretty much exactly 2 hours after leaving Crackington Haven I hopped over a stone style and turned off the path to the Boscastle Farm Shop and cafe. My plan had me entering the harbour in Boscastle over an hour later, so I was quite ahead of schedule at this point - this is what happens when I'm not being kept sensible by Chris! I refilled water bottles from the tap outside the cafe, and picked up another can of drink for a bit of flavour from the shop and headed on, noticing the bus stop which I assumed was where Chris would be heading away from in a few hours.

I rounded the headlands to see the classic view of Boscastle, a town made famous by catastrophic floods back in 2004. On 16th August, warm, moist air travelling in from the Atlantic Ocean dumped a phenomenal, unprecedented amount of rain in a very short time on the land above Boscastle. The torrential rain led to a 2-metre rise in river levels in *one hour*. Pooling debris trapped in the river held back water but eventually broke, leading to a 3m wave that flowed down into the village, part of the estimated 20 *million* tons of water that flowed through Boscastle on that day. 75 cars, 5 caravans, 6 buildings and several boats were washed away, with 100 homes destroyed. 7 Sea King helicopters rescued about 150 people clinging to trees, buildings and cars. By an amazing stroke of luck, no one was killed or seriously injured. If the date sounds familiar, it's because it was exactly 52 years *to the day* after the flood in Lynmouth, that I passed through on my first day, had claimed 34 lives.

Boscastle gets remembered for these floods as it got most of the national news attention, but Crackington Haven - where I was a couple of hours before - also suffered from the floods on that day. Twelve properties were flooded, 2 destroyed with cars, caravans and footbridges washed away.

I dropped down to Boscastle but didn't stop in the town, crossing the bridge and heading straight up the hill on route to Tintagel, by my estimations a little over 4 miles away. I was looking forward to getting there and still feeling good. We'd been on a family holiday in Bude a month previously and had visited Tintagel Castle for the day during which I'd made a mental note of where the path went through the area, but I hadn't explored any further north than the cafe and toilets at the bottom of the hill.

The route to Tintagel was green grass and heather with the sea visible for most of the way, and finally the grey clouds were moving on to make way for bright blue sky, lighting up the beach at Bossiney Haven with bright sunshine. I made a mistake close to the Tintagel of thinking I had to head further out towards the sea but I was starting to get a sense of when things were not quite

123

right navigation-wise and caught it early, although I would have fairly quickly run out of land if I'd kept going the wrong way.

You can always tell when you're nearing somewhere interesting by the number of people you see. When out in the middle of nowhere, you see the odd person or couple, usually in decent walking shoes, trousers and often with a pack on their back and a pole or two in their hands. As you approach landmarks, the type of person changes - family groups, people who don't look quite so comfortable walking, flip-flops, trainers, way-to-cool fashion gear and quite a few grumpy looking people obviously being dragged along by another member of their pack.

This was the case approaching Tintagel. I passed a progressively growing number of groups of people, rounded the last corner and could now see the new cantilever bridge entrance to the National Trust run castle high in the air in the distance. I made my way down a set of stony steps to the Beach Cafe area.

When we were there in August, the toilets were open but everything else at the lower end of Tintagel was closed. For some reason, they'd decided to open everything up now it was September and the kids were back at school, and the place was absolutely heaving. I'd hoped to get some water - I wasn't in desperate need, but as far as I knew this was the last stop before the end which was a good 8 or 9 miles away so figured heading out with 2 full bottles and my spare filled up would be a good idea. But with the queues for the cafe being at least 10 people deep I decided that wouldn't work. I tried the toilets but they had *Not Drinking Water* signs, and asked in the shop where they

124

suggested a cleaning cupboard with a tap in might be open. It wasn't, and to be fair I did have quite a bit of water - enough as long as it didn't get stupidly hot today - so I gave up and got on with walking.

It's always when you go through busy places that the paths get a bit more muddled, and I ended up taking a couple of wrong paths after climbing the hill out of Tintagel. It didn't make much difference, but it just gets a bit annoying when you're trying to make progress and keep having to turn around and walk a minute or two back in the other direction to take the right path. The views around Tintagel are phenomenal though, so spending a little extra time there wasn't a problem. Heading south as I was, you could see Pentire point in the distance, with various rocks and stacks visible out to sea around the local area.

I was thinking about drink and food in a fairly general sense when the realisation dawned on me that although I had some food in my pack, it was almost entirely snacks like flapjacks and liquorice allsorts - not the sort of thing I really wanted for dinner, so stopping on a bit of grass a mile short of Port Isaac seemed like a flawed plan. As the day was going well, it was an easy decision to change the plan, add a mile or so to the distance and head into the village. There, I would find supplies to load my pack up with and plenty of places for evening food, and it would be a better place to meet Chris than a random spot on the hill. I sent him a text message to update him of the plan.

I was approaching Trebarwith Strand. I could see the sand of the beach in the distance, but what I didn't expect was that

125

Trebarwith itself would be a little village with cafes and pubs. I could see all the tables outside the Port William pub on the far side of the beach as I came down the hill and heading into the final stretch picking out the Strand Cafe ahead.

With the promise of decent food at Port Isaac, I only wanted water so I went inside and asked if they could fill my bottles. Everywhere so far had been more than happy to do this, but here the lady behind the counter looked a little less than impressed and said I had to put a donation in the box. I've no problem with making a donation or even paying a bit for a water top up, after all someone is paying the bill for it. But the problem was I didn't have any cash other than notes and it seemed a bit much to pay £10 for a water top up. I asked if I could buy something instead, and she tutted but did take the bottles to fill. I ordered a can of coke from the other person serving, then had the bright idea of her charging me an extra £1 and then putting the pound from the till into the donation box, which turned out to actually exist (call me sceptical) - it was for the lifeguard service, a great cause. Happy with how it had all turned out, I headed out with 2 full bottles and a can of coke, the can in typical style lasting about 10 seconds.

Along the coast path, almost all the villages are in the valleys. This makes logical sense - access to the water was the main reason there was any sort of settlement there in the first place. But that means that each time you stop at a cafe, you then head straight back up, and in the case of Trebarwith it was quite a significant zig-zag hill, ending with a very steep stepped section up to the higher ground, definitely not a set of steps you want to fall on! Looking back from the top, the village looked a long way down, and a wall of fog was coming in from the sea so Tintagel had disappeared from sight. Chris, who is a very keen caver, had mentioned some sea caves and quarries around the south end of Trebarwith Strand and I kept a vague look out for them but as I passed by, I didn't manage to see anything from the path.

By this point, Port Isaac was visible in the distance. Remembering how long it took to get the 11 or 12 miles to Clovelly from when I first saw it in the distance, Port Isaac looked a lot further away than the 5 miles that my GPS implied it was, so I did wonder if maybe this was another town further along the coast. A quick check of the OS Maps on my phone showed there was only one place ahead, so it must have been the pair of villages - Port Gaverne and Port Isaac.

The ground initially was not too lumpy, but as I closed in on the destination things got significantly hillier. In the space of about 1 mile between Jacket's Point and Ranie Point there were 4 deep valleys, dropping from close to 300ft down to almost sea level, the final one rising to over 400ft. This coincided with my usual waning after about 25 miles of walking, so I was getting a little less impressed with the fairly significant descents and then immediate reciprocal ascents.

Things flattened out in the last mile to Port Gaverne where I passed by some nice-looking houses and down a road towards the town. The SWCP branched off to the left down a final steep valley and then I headed up the road into Port Isaac at just around 5:30pm.

Chris had messaged to say his bus was due at around 6:30pm, so I had some time to kill and I was hungry. I passed a nice-looking place on the left as I entered Port Isaac, but I felt my "Stinky Walker" look was many levels of respectability below the requirement for that place so I walked on. I was looking out for a shop to buy things for my pack for the next day, but all I could find were trinket shops and ice cream places, all of which were in the process of closing or already closed. Further down the hill, I reached the Golden Lion pub that I'd been heading for, hoping for a spot inside. I should have learnt by now really, but I was met with a sign on the door saying they were full at the moment and to check back later.

At this point I started to get a bit annoyed with the whole situation. 30 miles into the day, all I wanted was simple food, snacks etc for my pack, and some basic grub for dinner to fill up what I'd burnt off - was that too much to ask? What I was faced with was a pretty village that was - as far as I was concerned - absolutely useless. It was entirely my fault for not planning these details obviously, but it didn't stop me from thinking the whole place was bloody ridiculous! I guess Doc Martin's grumpiness is contagious around Portwenn[7]... I mean Port Isaac.

_____

[7] The British TV series Doc Martin is about a grumpy doctor who develops haemophobia - the fear of blood - and moves to

Carrying on down the road I rounded the corner of the pub and saw a queue to an outside bar at the back so I joined the back of the line for the Mote Bar and Cafe. At least a beer would have some calories and be something to enjoy. As I waited in the queue, the internet connection to the place went down (I'm not sure if it was just the pub or the whole village), so they couldn't take cards anymore and were only accepting cash - a strange concept in Covid times where everything had switched over to contactless payments to reduce people touching anything.

At the front of the queue, I enquired about food options and the guy said they had a very limited menu of just fish and chips. Fine by me, as that was exactly what I was after, so I excitedly ordered a portion, along with a pint of Atlantic IPA and a glass of tap water. It came to £17, but I didn't argue and just paid up. I had to go back into my bag to get more cash out and part with a twenty, wondering for a moment if there were any cash points around the village but quickly dismissing them as far too useful a thing to have here. The guy disappeared off to get my change, eventually coming back with it and one of those buzzy things that tell you when your food is ready, and then proceeded to serve the next customer until I reminded him he owed me a beer and glass of water as well. "Ahhh, yes! Sorry!" He disappeared again, and came back with the beer. I gave up on the idea of the water from here, wished the next guy in the queue good luck and walked over

the seaside village of Portwenn. While Portwenn is fictional, the series is filmed on location in Port Isaac.

to a boat on the slipway which I propped myself up against in the absence of anywhere else to sit, while I sipped my IPA and waited for the buzzer to buzz.

Five minutes later it started skittering around on the ground and flashing so I pulled myself up using the boat and, like a man who's just walked 30 miles, wobbled my way over to a rather chaotic scene of lots of people grabbing their fish and chips. I got mine, rather unimpressed with the look of the plain white cardboard box for the £12 it had cost me.

Sitting back down by my boat (I'd decided I quite liked it at this point), I opened up my box. It looked good... very good. And it was indeed a very decent fish and chips. Really nice cod, lovely batter, sprinkled with what looked like samphire and chives and very nicely cooked chips - I can highly recommend the fish and chips from the Mote Bar in Port Isaac, as long as you don't mind paying 12 quid for it. And the Atlantic IPA was also very much appreciated after the long day's walking, but I already knew you couldn't go far wrong with a Sharp's beer.

I finished the fish and chips, popped the various bits and pieces into their appropriate bins back by the pub and wandered down with the remains of my pint to the sea, finding a nice wall to sit on.

I had nothing to do but sit, sip beer and wait for Chris to get here. I took the opportunity to call my sister, Niki, who I hadn't spoken to for a few days and we had a good chat about how things were going. A few minutes later, Chris appeared having seen me sitting on the wall while he walked down the hill from the bus stop. I finished the call with Niki and then Chris and I caught up about our respective trips, grumbled a bit about the pub being full and then headed up to the Old School which Chris had noticed on his walk down earlier. They had space and were serving food, so we got a table outside in the pleasant evening, another pint each and despite having only eaten fish and chips 30 minutes earlier I got myself a second dinner of burger and chips - I would have preferred a jacket potato but the menu was quite limited. I would rather err on the side of eating too much rather than too little from now on, although, again, those two meals combined probably accounted for less than half of what I burnt that day.

Another half pint each and some water, the bill paid up (by phone this time - they obviously had internet at the top of the village), we donned our packs and headed back down past the Golden Lion and onto Roscarrock Hill up and out the other side of Port Isaac to start looking for a camping spot.

It was pretty dark at this time. We stopped half way up the hill and took a couple of photos with our phones back down towards the harbour, taking the opportunity to show Chris how to use the Night Mode on his phone camera. It turns out we were pretty much directly outside Fern Cottage - probably better known as Doc Martin's house in the TV series - but we had our backs to it and it was dark so we didn't notice.

With head torches on we carried on up the road which then turned into the coast path track. Although not visible, the sea was clearly audible on the right side as we walked on the grassy ground. We went through a gate to an area that looked potentially suitable for camping, but the ground above - before the gate - was flatter and more suited. We were about a mile out of town, and there were a few sheep in the field, but it seemed like public ground rather than anyone's field and we were both tired, so we settled down there. I was in a much better place mentally than when I did my previous bit of wild camping two nights before back on the outskirts of Braunton, and I figured at least if we could get some hours sleep there would be a lot more potential spots along this stretch of path if we got moved on for any reason.

It took the usual half an hour or so to get everything set up, stopping for a moment when a dog started barking in the background. We waited to check that it wasn't a local or, worse, a farmer coming in our direction, and when satisfied it wasn't we carried on quietly setting up tents and inflating mats. A bit of clothes changing in the tent, a joke about hoping the sheep don't get attracted to the warmth of the tent and sit on us in the night (at least I think it was a joke), and that was us done for the day.

As I lay in the tent relaxing after a hard day's walk, I could hear gentle footsteps outside the tent and the munching of the grass. Knowing the sheep were about, rather than being concerned about the noises I found them quite comforting and drifted asleep, occasionally being lightly woken by their rustling outside through the night.

CHAPTER 8

Day 6: Port Isaac to Padstow (then bus to Newquay)

Shipping containers, fish & chips and an open-top bus ride.

Start Time	**6:33am**
Total Distance	**15.62 miles + approx. 1 mile (watch not running)**
Elevation	**2662 feet**
Total Time	**9 hours 13 mins**
Moving Time	**4 hours 48 mins (18:28mins/mile)**
Steps	**44135**

The sunrise was getting later each day, the mornings were darker, and on this particular one we were slightly concerned about Farmer Giles appearing with a double-barrelled shotgun to kick us off his land. It was pretty dark when my watch buzzed at 5:50am, and after the usual in-tent pack down of sleeping gear I poked my head outside to see another tent at the far side of the same field - a popular spot!

On my carefully crafted plan, today had me walking to Rock, crossing the river Camel to Padstow on the ferry then continuing another 20 miles or so on to around Mawgan Porth a little north of Newquay, making it a pretty long day of about 33 miles in total. But with the missed day between Clovelly and Bude, the original target of the whole coast path in 21 days was out of the question, and my annoyance at the logistics in Port Isaac last night had seeded the idea of relaxing the plan, easing back, skipping a few bits and most likely finishing early. After a good sleep last night, that seed had grown. Essentially, I'd decided I was going to do what I felt like, having some enjoyable easier days, rather than religiously stick to the plan.

With that in mind, we decided to make today a leisurely walk to Rock, head up to Sharp's brewery to have a pint of Doom Bar, then head over to Padstow to sample and rate Rick Stein's fish and chips. After that, we'd get a bus to Newquay which was a little past the original end point for the day.

We packed up quicker today. I finally felt like I was starting to get the hang of the order to pack things up and where to put them. We got going around 6:30am.

The path was back to the light gravel track cut into grassland, with headlands and valleys visible out into the distance under the damp, grey sky. We passed through Port Quin about an hour after starting, with Doyden Castle dominant atop one of the hills shortly after. Another half an hour later and we were at Lundy Bay admiring Lundy Hole, a collapsed sea cave leaving a natural arch that Chris was trying to decide whether kayaking through in the current fairly rough sea conditions would be a good idea. I thought not, but he decided it would be quite fun.

Around 9:30am at Pentire Point we got our first view of Polzeath beach in the distance, and 30 minutes later we headed up the steps at TJs Surf Cafe to see what we could get for breakfast. They did a nice cooked breakfast with toast and we both had the usual black coffee to wake ourselves up for the day. Heading off from the cafe, we went back up the road to the Spar shop and got a few snacks - crisps and drinks for later in case we needed them, although the day was now going to be through fairly built-up areas so it was unlikely that we'd have a desperate need for food or water from our packs.

As we walked towards Rock, I had another sudden and somewhat urgent need for the conveniences. With all the random timing, quantities and types of food I was eating along with the exercise, I think getting a bit caught out only twice in a whole week wasn't too bad. We were approaching town, so I wasn't too concerned about finding something, and soon at the north end of Daymer Bay there was a car park with toilets at the back.

Sometimes, though, things just aren't as easy as they should be. By now, it was getting a bit urgent and I was relieved to see the aforementioned toilets. The ladies were at the front with the disabled toilet next door but I couldn't see the gents. My heart sank as I realised there was a coin-operated lock on the front requiring something daft like 30p - I had no coins left at all! I guessed the gents would be the same, but the lock on the disabled looked a bit different so I went to have a look and found you could also use a contactless card. I tried Apple Pay on my phone. It didn't work. I tried again. Still no luck. And again. This was really, *really* not the time for things to be taking this long! I asked Chris if I could borrow a bank card as I knew he had one handy and just in case my phone was the cause of the problem, but still no luck. As a last resort, I went around the back of the building to where I hoped the gents would be, tried my phone there and *eureka!* It worked and the door opened! I think I'll end the story there, other than to mention that they had the oddest vacuum toilets in there - you had to lock the lid down and press the button which then made some sort of explosive sound and probably fired excrement across to Padstow or something. Well worth 30p if it did, I'd say.

After that little bit of excitement and relief, we walked down into Rock - the home of Sharp's Brewery where they make Doom Bar, Atlantic IPA and lots of other lovely beers. It would be rude not to visit, and Chris had it on good authority that they had a place to sit and charge phones so we headed off up the hill with me occasionally checking my phone to make sure we were going in the right direction.

It turns out Pityme - where the brewery is *actually* located - was a good half an hour walk from the ferry crossing which we needed to get back to in order to cross to Padstow and continue on the path, or at least continue to the fish and chip shop and a bus stop. As we walked up roads, more roads, and another road we were starting to think maybe it wasn't the greatest idea, but with it now "just round the corner" we had committed to this endeavour and were going to see it through! Finally, the big steel vats came into view, along with a huge black tank with DOOM BAR written along the side in faded white letters. A well-earned celebratory beer awaited us!

Or rather, it didn't.

The main door to the building was closed off, and at one end was a hatch with a short queue. Inside the hatch was a man with a mask on, serving pre-packed products from the brewery to take away. Now I do like a bottle of Doom Bar, but with 13kg already on my back I didn't fancy carrying a couple of mini kegs of the stuff in my hands as well, so despondently, we aborted. After some disappointed chatter about it not being open, especially considering the unexpectedly long walk up, we headed off again, continuing along the road we'd arrived on to take a slightly different route back down to Rock.

On the right was a van selling food, and just behind were a bunch of bright yellow shipping containers, one with the door open and filled with shiny vats, tubes and various pressure gauges. The sign said *Lowlands Brewing*. At the far end, one of the containers had a door, so we poked our heads in and stumbled upon the Taproom.

What a great little place! A bar in a shipping container, with tables and chairs inside - and plugs to charge our phones. 2 minutes up from the disappointment of Sharp's, we'd stumbled across this - another stroke of luck! They had a really interesting selection of beers on tap that they served in ⅓ and ⅔ pint options, so we tried a couple of them while having a chat with one of the guys who's place it was. They'd been there 6 months or so, starting with empty containers and kitting them out as the taproom and brewery and were about to start brewing properly having taken delivery of their kit recently. It was a really pleasant time, sitting and chatting with people who knew their stuff and were really excited about the potential of their business. I even learnt about double and triple IPAs, having a taste of their rather potent triple which was *dangerously* drinkable! Hopefully it all works out for them, and if you're in the area then do check them out - it's definitely worth it.

Time and tide wait for no man however, particularly relevant when you have a ferry to catch. We said goodbye and headed back onto the road down into Rock to try and make the ferry at 2pm when, apparently, they started up again after a lunch break, at least according to the info I had read on the website earlier. We passed road signs to places like Tredrizzick, Polzeath and Trebetherick, commenting on how it really was like being in a different country. Apparently, *tre* means settlement or

138

homestead, *pol* is a pond, lake or well and *pen* is a hill or headland and those 3 are very common in Cornish place names.

As we walked down into the town and could clearly see the Camel estuary… which was about 90% sand - it was fairly clear that no boat was going to be crossing that! I checked the timings of the boat on the board and they indicated it didn't start again until after 4pm, 2 hours from now. At the bottom of the timetable, a handwritten message pointed out there was another ferry half a mile further towards the sea, so we headed off and soon saw the queue of people walking across the sand. They'd either been for a mass swim, or had just come across from Padstow on the ferry.

Over the top of the sand bank, we caught sight of the little bright yellow Rock-Padstow ferry waiting. We joined the end of the queue, paid our £3 each and took a seat for the 2-minute crossing on the funky little flat-bottomed boat that zipped across to Padstow, landing at the superbly named Chiddleypump!

If Rock is known for Sharp's brewery, then Padstow is known for Rick Stein. He's got 3 restaurants and a fish and chip shop in the town, and Chris was keen to try the latter out and see if the classic English takeaway met expectations. We'd been having a discussion about what would make a fish and chip shop really good. Everyone who's been to their local fish and chip shop a few times knows that the quality can vary - the fryers don't want to waste food, so you sometimes get the crispy little ends of the chips, or a bit of fish that's been kept warm for a bit too long and is drier than it could be. To be considered really good as the reputation suggested, we figured Rick Stein's place would have to serve great fish and chips every time as most people were likely just passing through so would only try them once. We were keen to find out if we were right.

The coast path took us through a rapidly growing number of people to a packed Padstow Harbour area with several fish and chips shops. A quick check of the map and we headed down Riverside to Rick Stein's gaff. There was quite a queue outside, but unlike my local fish and chip shop they were very efficient so it didn't take long to get our order in - 2 haddock and chips. Standing outside with a buzzer doodah again, we sorted various bits out in our bags and took advantage of the toilets in the area, and soon were called up to get our fodder. We sat on a planter in the car park and ate. I know you're absolutely *desperate* to know what we thought... right? Well, I'd rate them as very good to excellent fish and chips - certainly not a disappointment at all. Like at the Mote in Port Isaac, the fish was tender, moist and full of flavour and the batter crispy but not overcooked. The chips were really good too, but Chris thought they were cooked in a different oil to usual and tasted a bit odd. Not bad, but different. I'm not sure I could taste the difference to be honest - they were crispy on the outside, soft in the middle, not greasy, and tasted very nice. So good work, Mr Stein!

Just across the road from where we sat, there was a rapidly growing queue at a bus stop and as an open-top bus turned up we concluded that was the one for us. The *Atlantic Coaster* would be taking us on a scenic route to Newquay. We queued for a bit, got on and paid the standard £6 each (it seems it's either £4.80 or £6 for a single trip anywhere in Cornwall) and headed up to the top deck, squeezing ourselves and packs into a free spot right at the back.

The bus route was very scenic once we were on the coast. We went through Porthcothan, Treburrick and fairly close to the actual end point on my plan around Bedruthan Steps. Further down past Mawgan Porth, the airport was the dominant feature inland. I was meeting Howard tomorrow morning to walk a section of the path together, but right now he was at work in the airport and as I passed by on the bus I looked across at the terminal building, wondering what he was up to in there.

We didn't have any accommodation booked but despite it being a Friday night in what we now knew was a seriously overbooked Cornwall, we were hoping to find a spot in a campsite in Newquay. A search on the OS map app gave us a few possibilities that we should pass close by on the bus so we could scope them from a distance if they were likely to be suitable for tents. As we passed the first it looked very much like a caravan-only site, and the next we ended up not being able to see from the bus route.

We went past the train station at Newquay where Chris would be heading off in the morning, tinged the bell and got off on the main street in town. This spot was near to the Tourist Information Centre (TIC) where we were heading in the hope they might be able to phone and find us a spot for the night.

We explained our situation to the guy in the TIC - he wasn't hopeful. He said that in Newquay, most campsites had a rule that they wouldn't allow any all-male groups as it was a haven for stag dos and I imagine they've seen their fair share of noise and trouble from groups. I did point out that we were two separate hikers with our own tents, but he didn't seem very confident. He started with the nearest one - Trenance Holiday Park. The phone conversation quickly turned positive and within a couple of minutes he had us a pitch booked for the two tents at the princely sum of £10 each. Fantastic! I was very relieved, it's so much nicer knowing you have a decent place to kip, with wash facilities and a shower to clean up and the town just down the road to get some good food. All we had to do was get there before reception shut at 5pm. Looking at my watch I saw we had 10 minutes, so we thanked the guy and got on our way.

We headed up a fairly big hill and then down another to the campsite, paid up at the reception before they closed, bought some tokens for the showers and headed up another hill to our pitch at the back of the site. It was perfect - flat ground, not noisy, plenty of space. We both set up our tents quickly and easily, had showers and changed into something vaguely respectable. For me, that was the pair of running tights which were kept as my cold-weather gear so hadn't been used for walking, my lightweight waterproof trousers which actually looked fairly close to normal trousers, and a black long-sleeved merino top, again part of my unworn cold-weather gear. I also stuck on my down jacket as it was going to get dark and likely a little colder. We tucked our packs under the outer sheets of our tents. Unlike that day in Dorchester where I worried some nice lady would be off with my pack in 2 minutes, I was now happy to leave it for an evening in a campsite full of people. Attitude and priorities change when you've been on the road for a while. And besides, good luck to anyone who nicked that pack and its contents - I think technically it should probably have been classed as a bioweapon by this point!

We headed into town, taking it slowly up and down the hills. Our legs were feeling tired, and Chris was starting to have considerable issues with his feet in the boots but was happy to walk along if we kept it slow. We hit the main street again, wandering along among a lot of hyped-up people. Friday night in Newquay was obviously a busy place, with a lot of people looking like they were building up to a heavy night. There were some vaguely appealing looking places, which to us meant not covered in neon, flashing lights and pumping out loud dance music - but most places were really busy even at not much past 6pm. At the far end of town, we settled on a bar that had space, picked an outside table that wasn't reserved and ordered a burger and chips each and the obligatory pint.

"Not too busy" soon turned into "a very noisy group of blokes getting progressively more shouty", and then the waitress came out and told us the group had reserved the table we were sitting on, despite it not having any sign on. Obviously, the big group was going to spend a lot more money than us in here, so the two weirdly dressed people that smelt a bit odd were getting politely turfed out - makes perfect sense to be fair. We finished up and headed off just as one of the guys knocked a glass out of the hand of another accidentally, sending glass and beer crashing down all over the ground and triggering some heated conversation between the pair that had the bouncers at the gate paying attention as we left. The perfect time to leave I think!

There was a Wetherspoons on the route back to the campsite and as this trip had inadvertently turned into a crawl of all Wetherspoons in Somerset, Devon and Cornwall it seemed rude not to continue the trend, so we called in there and ordered a pint of Doom Bar each.

It was at this point that I pushed the button and committed to my return home.

I'd spent a bit of time looking at how to get home. I'd started with the idea of taking the bus part way across Cornwall to a train station somewhere with decent connections, but that idea got complicated and the trip was looking like it would take a very long time. Then I looked at coaches out of Penzance - the only route suggested took over 11 hours via London Victoria and then down to Bournemouth, er… no, I'm not sitting on coaches for 11 hours! As a last resort I checked the train, expecting it to be ridiculously expensive. Again, the route suggested out of Penzance back to Poole was silly with loads of changes, lots of waiting and as expected costing over £100. I played around a bit shortening the journey to sections, and found I could get one train to Exeter, and then from Exeter to Salisbury was one train too. Putting that lot into the app came out at what now felt like a very decent £36! My sister lives in Salisbury, and it's not too far to get back home from there.

I checked my dates - my plan had me in Penzance on Monday evening. I double checked, gave it one last thought to make sure I was happy to end this adventure early, then hit the button and bought my ticket home for Tuesday morning out of Penzance.

Pints finished, we headed back through the streets of town to the campsite and settled in for another decent night's sleep. I was finally beginning to get the hang of this tenting malarkey.

CHAPTER 9

Day 7: Newquay to Camborne

Mines, you say? Oh, go on then, add another 12 miles.

Start Time	**8:03am**
Total Distance	**29.75 miles**
Elevation	**4125 feet**
Total Time	**8 hours 48 mins**
Moving Time	**7 hours 44 mins (15:36mins/mile)**
Steps	**59566**

Today was the day I'd be saying goodbye to Chris. The timing was perfect for him as his feet were ruined from all the walking, and the superglue on his boots had held up so far but was showing signs it probably wasn't going to last much longer[8].

With my alarm set for a leisurely 7am, I woke a little earlier to the sound of seagulls calling and flying around the site which was actually a really nice way to wake. I had a leisurely wash in the block, still feeling like it was a luxury compared with either nothing or splashing my face in a cafe toilet! With my tear-down routine now pretty well established and the sun usefully above the horizon, everything was down and in the pack in no time at all.

Throughout the evening yesterday I'd been messaging back and forth with Howard and he was coming to the campsite for 8am. Just before then, I wished Chris a good journey home and we said our goodbyes and with some sadness I headed down to the reception of the campsite. Chris joining me had been unplanned, and I wasn't sure how it was going to go. But it was superb! Despite not having seen each other for quite a few years, we got on really well, conversation was easy and when it came to decisions about the trip, we were both on the same wavelength. It was a real pleasure spending the best part of a week with him on this walk.

---

[8] Since finishing the path walk, those boots have done a good chunk more walking, including around Portland. So maybe pack a pot of superglue in your kit bag, just in case!

Tonight, I had a room booked at the Premier Inn in Camborne - my first actual bed in 7 days - and I was hugely looking forward to it. It was also one of the most expensive rooms I've ever stayed in. Eva booked it for me as a treat and told me not to argue, but at almost £200 for a single night in a Premier Inn you can get a sense of how madly busy Cornwall was! To put this in context, I've used this hotel when doing the Arc of Attrition race and in early February the price was just over £25 per night.

To make sure I made the most of this ridiculously expensive room, I wanted to get to Camborne for the check-in time of 4pm. I'd spent some time looking at the route for today and had 2 potential end points. There was a bus from Perranporth at around 12 miles in at 2:25pm, or if I made it there really early and was feeling good, I could go on another 6 miles to St Agnes and catch another bus from there around 2:30pm. Both busses went to Threemilestone, then there was one from there to the hotel in Camborne, arriving just before 4pm. I'd just have to see how things went for the day and decide which one to catch.

I first met Howard about 10 years ago when he was a photographer living in Swanage. We were part of a local informal photography related group that got together, generally at a pub, and waffled on about anything and everything. He moved to Cornwall a good few years ago and was now living on the outskirts of Newquay. I hadn't seen him for probably 6 years, but we'd stayed in touch online and as soon as we got together conversation just flowed. I love it when it's like that, when you can just pick up where you left off even after years.

We headed off out the campsite, me with my pack and walking poles and Howard with an over-the-shoulder messenger style bag loaded with flasks of coffee and what looked like a pair of sandals on his feet. His plan was to walk with me as long as he felt comfortable, so we just went off to see what would happen.

The first thing to do was to cross the river Gannel. There are 4 ways to do this, 3 of them depend on the tide and one is longer, going around on the road. Unfortunately, we were pretty much at the highest tide of the day, and although as we walked along the road and looking at the crossing saw it was only about 10% submerged, we both knew that further up the path was another crossing that was likely to be completely under water so it wasn't really worth stripping off shoes etc to wade the first part, only to have to turn around at the second.

The road option is normally quite a bit of extra walking, but with the location of the campsite being a fair distance inland from the coast path already we were actually in a position where a good chunk of that extra distance had been covered. We walked around on the pavement of the main A road to cross the road bridge over the river, then turned on to a smaller road and headed to Crantock, where we joined the coast path just past the second (potentially underwater) crossing.

Howard was great to walk with. Initially I had thought he looked like he was off for a gentle stroll around town with his bag and sandals, but right from the start we were heading along the roads at a great pace. The conversation was easy and constant, we spent a long while discussing nutrition, healthy eating and mindfulness, interspersed with Howard's local knowledge adding commentary on various points of interest that were around us.

We passed around Pentire Point[9] and got a great view of Porth Joke (also known as Poly Joke) beach, the word Joke coming from the Cornish *lojowek* meaning "cove abounding in vegetation". Howard was explaining stories about the areas as we passed, and a little further down was Holywell. Here, down at sea level, there were a set of steps cut into the rocks of the cliff and over a long period of time of water flowing down them they ended up covered in calciferous deposits called flowstone. The water still trickles down the steps pooling in various areas, with beautiful mineral colours on the rocks behind. The tide was in so we couldn't go around to see the area, but it's a place I'd like to visit in the future.

Crossing the back of Holywell beach on the coast path, it turned out access to the beach was restricted anyway. There was some sort of filming in progress and security people were stopping anyone from going onto the beach. A bit of a look on the internet suggests it may have been something to do with a prequel to *Game of Thrones*.

---

[9] *Pentire* in Cornish means *promontory*, defined as "a point of high land that juts out into the sea or a large lake; a headland". This explains why we passed Pentire Point Polzeath *and* again just after Newquay.

After passing the beach at Holywell, the path went slightly inland and as it was a little after 10am I was ready to get some breakfast. Just off the beach, we came across Gull Rocks bar and coffee house. They didn't have an option for a full breakfast, but on a sign hidden a little out of view there was the option of bacon, sausage or egg baps. Not ideal, but that would do.

I went inside and ordered a sausage bap with an added egg along with a black coffee from a quite stern lady that seemed more annoyed at having to take my order than anything else. At this point, I wasn't expecting much, but it was food and I was hungry.

A few minutes later outside at the table, my coffee arrived. I drink a lot of coffee, and have made my own espresso-based beverages for years. While I'm not hugely picky, I can tell you this one was over extracted, bitter and not great but it had caffeine and that was primarily what I was after. It didn't improve my expectations for the food.

Then the bap turned up. Oh boy… What a bap! A fantastic soft brioche bun, and perfectly cooked egg with a lovely running middle, 2 really tasty sausages and topped off with a single hash brown on the side of the plate. Definitely the best breakfast bun I've ever had, more than making up for the coffee! I can *highly* recommend nipping into the Gull Rocks to grab one if you're passing in the morning, even if the lady at the till seems a little preoccupied!

We carried on walking, chatting about the military use of the local area. I knew something of the chemical weapons development at Portreath, but Howard talked of various local discussions about secret submarine communications bases on land, and disguised radar installations along the coast. It got me excited to keep a lookout for unusual things near the path, and guess the stories behind them.

Not long after Holywell, we rounded the corner along another stretch of path that felt slightly precarious - the path itself was fine, but step to the right and you'd be on a steep grass slope that disappeared off a cliff at its bottom end. Further along and away from the edge, we went down a steep, rough and winding slope onto the north end of Perran Sands with Perranporth in the distance. Howard's knees were starting to play up and he didn't much enjoy the descent onto the beach, but once down it was firm flat sand and we both headed along happily. It was just before 11:30am, so I was a long way ahead of my timing for the bus, even with a few more miles to walk on the sand.

We walked along, discussing the jellyfish on the beach. There were a lot of the clear ones (Moon jellyfish I think) which Howard said were fine to pick up. There were brown Compass jellyfish, which he *didn't* advise picking up, the sting is similar to stinging nettles. And although we didn't see any, he did mention that Portuguese Man O' War (which are not a jellyfish but a *siphonophore*, a collection of organisms) get washed up on the beach and you really, *definitely* should stay away from those!

The beach was flat, and like most Cornish beaches has a huge tidal range. The tide hadn't long gone out, leaving a lot of shallow pools of water on the sand. Howard's sandal-like footwear -

which turned out to be really decent Merrell open walking shoes - came into its own along here too. He could just walk through all the pools on the beach, while I had to bounce around on the little sand flats trying to avoid the water. At one point when I was talking too much and not concentrating on where I was going, I put my foot right in a deep hole, soaking it through, with me swearing and Howard laughing. The day was warm and dry though, and I knew with my merino socks on it wouldn't even feel wet in 5 minutes.

As we entered Perranporth at the far end of the beach, Howard pointed out the fencing and setup for an event on the beach. This was *Bands in the Sands*, where that evening bands would be performing on the beach with the Atlantic Ocean crashing away in the background. Howard also mentioned that he was off to do work at the *Eden Sessions* a little time later, where bands like *Royal Blood*, *Snow Patrol* and various were playing at the famous Eden Project - now *that* sounded like something I'd love to go along to! Not meaning to sound like the Cornish Tourist Board, but there really is a huge number of things to do there, and I must come back and explore more of Cornwall at a more leisurely rate in future.

We came off the beach at almost exactly 12pm, having covered 12 miles. I felt really good, both physically and mentally, and there was no way I was going to wait for over 2 hours for a bus but instead I'd carry on walking. Howard's feet had had enough for the day and we'd reached the furthest point he intended to get to anyway, so after a great time walking we said our goodbyes. While he headed off to get his lift back home, I got going on towards St Agnes, feeling very happy and thoroughly enjoying myself.

Coming out of Perranporth, the terrain quickly changed significantly into the kind of stuff I love, both to look at and walk over. Hard granite, great lumps of the stuff everywhere, with sideways strata rising up out of the ground. Underfoot, the stones were like small, loose gravel, the terrain spotted with bracken and heather here and there. Into the distance, the relatively flat surface of the land was peppered with steep drops and climbs where it met coves and beaches.

At Trevellas Cove, less than an hour out of Perranporth, I saw what I'd been waiting for - the first mine engine house! I have a real fascination with these things. Squat buildings with great chimneys rising up, like an iceberg just giving a hint of what lies beneath the ground. You can feel the history in these areas, see the remnants of the immense work that went on, and feel echoes of the power of both earth and machine. I just love this bit of the world! It seems I'm not the only one as great chunks of Cornwall are designated part of the Cornish Mining World Heritage Site.

An idea had been kicking around in my brain, and with this beautiful landscape now shouting at me to continue, I committed. Forget the bus, I was going to walk all the way to Camborne. I reckoned that would add 10-12 miles on to my original plan, but I didn't care. I was having a fantastic day, feeling really good, and I was finally in my favourite place - mining country!

154

As I passed St Agnes Head and headed towards Chapel Porth, the mines and engine houses were coming thick and fast. The path was cut into the granite, with cliffs and sea to the right, and colourful heather and bracken to the left. In the distance, the chimneys rose.

At about 2:30, I dropped down into Porthtowan.

Porthtowan has a special meaning to me - and to anyone else who's competed in the MudCrew *Arc of Attrition*. The Arc is a non-stop 100-mile race following the South West Coast Path from Coverack in south Cornwall (about 10 miles on the path east of the Lizard), round Land's End, past St Ives and along to the end at Porthtowan. In itself, that's a challenging distance over tough and varied terrain, but to add to the "entertainment", it takes place at the end of January. More than 13 hours of darkness, cold weather, wind, rain, possibly snow and ice add to the toughness, but make it an epic adventure!

I've started this race 3 times before. I've yet to finish it. My best effort got me as far as Pendeen, just under 70 miles in about 17 hours, but for two consecutive years I suffered from the same knee injury that ended my race. Even though the start is in Coverack, the HQ for the race is in Porthtowan, so I was fairly familiar with the area. And one of my goals I'd set myself for the adventure was to get onto the Arc course and soak up some of the atmosphere again.

So here I was, back in Porthtowan. I called into the village store and picked up a can of drink, only to be told I had to spend more to pay by card, so I bought 2 cans of drink and did my usual of downing one outside the shop, then putting the other in my pack.

I still felt physically and mentally good and headed up the fairly long and steep hill out of Porthtowan, squeezing in several times to avoid cars going in both directions on the very narrow road. Rounding the corner, I was back on the path proper and passing various derelict building works that looked part mine, part military. It got me thinking back to the conversation with Howard - maybe these were remains of some sort of secret underground base?

There's an album I listened to on repeat when I was mid-race in 2019, running through the night, skipping boulders at Lamorna, and singing out loud on the descent to Porthcurno. The pure emotion of my enjoyment became linked to that music, and whenever I put it on, I'm transported back to that time, seeing in my mind a circle of light from my headtorch revealing rocks, drops, cliffs and the sea. I try not to listen to it much now so as not to dilute the connection, but what better time to stick it on than back on the Arc course? I pulled the MP3 player out of the shoulder strap of my pack, extracted it from the dog-poo-bag I was using to waterproof it in case of rain, and dialled up *Amo* by *Bring Me the Horizon*.

A little further along (I believe at a place called Sally's Bottom) was a set of pretty brutal steps that went down and down, to come straight up and up again on the other side. Fairly typically for coast path steps, they were cut into the hill, and a wooden board formed the front of each step. Also fairly typically, over time a lot of the earth filling each step had worn away, making each step a big hole with a wooden trip hazard in front of it, not the nicest thing to descend at the best of time. Slowly and carefully is the way to do it, otherwise there's a fair chance of an unplanned rapid and uncontrolled descent!

My energy was just beginning to wane for the first time so far with more than 20 miles in my legs, which made me think of food. I remembered the trouble I had getting food in Port Isaac, so I got my phone out, found the number and called the hotel to book myself a spot in the restaurant, happy that I'd remembered and now had guaranteed food tonight.

A little further on, I came to the corner of RRH Portreath. This disused airfield is now a radar station (RRH stands for Remote Radar Head), and as I alluded to earlier, this place has an interesting and quite sinister history.

Built in 1940 as RAF Portreath, it served various purposes during the war and was handed back to the government from the RAF in 1950. The base then reverted to the local name of *Nancekuke* and became an outstation of the Chemical Defence Engineering laboratories at Porton Down (near Salisbury), primarily producing deadly nerve agents. Around 20 tons of Sarin gas were produced over the following decades (Sarin was notably used in the 1995 Tokyo subway attack), but the site also produced VX and mustard gas as well - all of these the stuff that you really, really don't want to get anywhere near. The site was mothballed and finally shut down in the 1980s. But investigations by the media in the early 2000s found that over the time the site was active, several workers died from exposure to nerve agents, and that toxic materials and much of the production equipment had just been dumped in nearby mineshafts. A multi-million-pound clean-up of the area started in 2003 following an extensive environmental assessment, but in 2006 a digger driver accidentally found equipment containing an irritant that could damage eyes, lungs and skin. The general feeling among locals is that there is a lot of secrecy and cover up in this area and it's maybe not quite as clean as the MOD might suggest...

As fascinating as I found the history of the area, I didn't necessarily want to hang around too much for obvious reasons! Also, the terrain was good for fast walking, so I motored on.

I dropped down in Portreath around 3:30pm, less than an hour after climbing up out of Porthtowan - not at all bad for a smidge under 4 miles with steep steps and a few hills! I was stocked with water so didn't need to stop and just carried on through the town and out, up steps and then another fair climb on grass onto the headland above Portreath.

My GPS had separate tracks for each day, so I knew where the planned end point for this day was but obviously it was a point on the coast path, not at the hotel. I'd spent a little time looking at the OS Maps of the area and found a footpath that ran pretty much straight from the coast path to Treswithian on the outskirts of Camborne where the hotel was located. But until I got to that turning off the path, I wasn't quite sure how far it was between the coast path and the hotel, my guess was a little over a mile.

A couple of miles of fast, flat walking later, I was beginning to wane and looking forward to getting onto the final stretch into town. I found the town-bound path to the left and pressed some buttons on my GPS to plot a path to the hotel, not because it was a difficult route but more because it would show me the distance I had remaining. It turned out to be 2.25 miles, which was further than I thought. An extra mile or so doesn't sound much considering the distance I was walking each day, but when you're tired and really looking forward to getting to a comfortable room, have a bath and chill out, adding an unexpected 15-20 minutes was irritating!

The path went out through a car park, across a fast but not too busy road and over a stone style into a field. I went through more gates and about 4 more fields, with the path getting narrower and more overgrown, continuously dropping downhill until the tiny hamlet of Coombe. Round a couple of corners that I was taking note of for the return leg tomorrow morning, and then I was on the final continuous uphill road that just seemed to go on and on, straight and up. I kept the pace up despite it feeling like hard work, knowing the faster I walked the quicker I'd be at the end. I met a road crossing where the route finally flattened out, and soon I was at the big raised junction with the A30, the Premier Inn in sight a few hundred metres away. I had to walk round 3 sides of the hotel building and attached pub to get around to the entrance, but at 4:52pm I walked through the front door and grinned like a Cheshire cat - time to relax!

I was glad to stop walking, but it had been a brilliant day. A few hours chatting with Howard, a few more in my favourite type of terrain with mines and engine houses, then going through areas I was actually familiar with now. A little under 9 hours after setting off I'd completed the 30 miles from Newquay to Camborne.

I waited my turn, then checked in with the lady at reception. We got chatting, and when I mentioned the reason for my pack and poles she asked if I was doing it for charity, and said she couldn't sponsor me but disappeared off to the back room and came back with a box of *Quality Street* chocolates for me - that was a lovely thing to do! I headed off to my room, took my pack off, opened the box and immediately munched 4 or 5 sweets and they tasted *great*!

After 7 days of camping, I had to figure out what to do when I had a table, chair, kettle, bed, TV, bathroom and all those luxuries that in everyday life you don't appreciate that you have. First things first - I got all the gadgets out plugged as much as I could in to charge. Then I started the bath taps running. I'm normally a shower person, but I wasn't going to pass up an opportunity to soak in a hot bath after all those days walking.

While the bath was filling, I took a risk and washed a few of my clothes in the sink. It wasn't a hot room, but I was hoping that it would be warm enough for things to dry by morning - particularly my compression shorts which I'd need to be wearing tomorrow.

The bath was as soothing as expected, and I spent the time laying there replying to various social media comments and writing some blurb about the day.

Soon it was time for dinner in the pub. I had a prawn cocktail starter (I haven't had prawn cocktail for years!), and a lovely steak pie for main, all washed down with a couple of Doom Bar's.

While I sat, I wrote a whole load of notes about the previous few days - notable things that had happened, and reminders of key events. I also spent some time looking at bus timetables to come up with a plan for tomorrow.

According to The Plan, I was to go on to Cape Cornwall. Eva had booked me a camping spot at the Land's End YHA which was pretty much perfectly situated just a couple of hundred metres from the endpoint of the day. To get there, however, I'd be doing the infamous St Ives to Pendeen section, a notoriously slow 12–13-mile section of coast that had lots of rough ground, boulders, hills and wet ground.

On top of that, the day from my original start location totalled just under 33 miles, but that original start location was now around 4 miles walk from my hotel as it was a little further along the coast path than where I'd turned off to get here. I was having trouble seeing myself doing 37 miles with a tough 13 miles in the middle without leaving very early in the morning, and to be quite honest I wanted to make the most of the ridiculously expensive hotel room!

So, I changed the plan. I'd get a bus to St Ives, leaving at 9:35am the next morning from pretty much across the road from the hotel. That would cut my day length down to closer to 20 miles with a later start, but keeping in the tough section which I really wanted to walk along. I would be missing out on what from memory was a fairly dull section through Hayle to St Ives which I'd walked back in 2018 with my cousin, but I would also sadly miss Godrevy head which I had really wanted to see. Oh well, just another excuse to come back later.

With that plan in place, after dinner I headed back to the reception and now that I was leaving later rather than at the crack of dawn, I booked a breakfast for the next morning. I headed off to my room, tidied a few things up and settled into what felt like the most comfortable bed I'd ever laid in.

CHAPTER 10
Day 8: St Ives to St Just

Zennor - home to the toughest of people: a retired lady with dodgy knees, one walking stick and a determination to get out on that roughest of paths...

Every.

Single.

Day.

Start Time	**10:15am**
Total Distance	**20.07 miles**
Elevation	**4037 feet**
Total Time	**7 hours 22 mins**
Moving Time	**5 hours 39 mins (16:53mins/mile)**
Steps	**40096**

The bed may have felt comfortable, but I didn't sleep all that well. I think I was getting used to sleeping in a tent on an inflatable mattress, and the comfort of a real mattress and duvet messed with my head a bit. I tossed and turned all night, never quite being in the right position, and always either too warm, too cold, or too wrapped up in the duvet.

The alarm buzzed at 7am and I got up and made coffee with the little in-room tea-and-coffee making facilities, which was a nice treat. While the caffeine slowly woke my head up, I checked on the washing that was hanging in the bathroom to find it was still quite a bit damper than I would have liked. I had a look around for things that I might be able to use to help them dry and rigged up a sort-of airing cupboard affair by hanging my clothes on the hangers in the open wardrobe area, then hanging the hairdryer on the front hanger and jamming the switch on with a compression clip from my bag. The result was hot air blowing around inside the wardrobe area, in theory drying my clothes. After 10 minutes I decided I'd better stop before the hair dryer caught fire (I wouldn't have thought the little plastic hairdryers in Premier Inns are meant to be run for too long at a time), and when checking the compression shorts, I found they were now warm and damp instead of cold and damp. Hey ho, it was worth a try.

Just before 8am, I stuck on my standard "formal attire" of waterproof trousers and the black long-sleeved top - the one that I hadn't worn walking so didn't smell of dead badger like everything else I possessed - and headed on down to breakfast.

Premier Inn breakfasts are a bit of a favourite thing for my family (we're easy to please). You pay about £9 and can eat whatever you like from the buffet - perfect when you're walking hundreds of miles. The only spanner in this plan was that I wasn't feeling very hungry, which was bloody annoying! I still managed to have a fairly full plate of sausages, eggs, mushrooms, black pudding, beans and bacon with a couple of slices of toast and butter, then force in a croissant and pain au chocolat afterwards. I was a bit disappointed with my effort though - my initial vision was of me strutting out the door in slow motion, leaving astounded staff contemplating a completely bare buffet area left behind.

I went back to the room, packed everything of mine that was lying around into my pack and headed off out. I got to the bus stop at 9:20am, with 15 minutes to wait. One thing about busses in Devon and Cornwall is that they may not be all that frequent, but they really do seem to be on time (obviously except for that one a while back where we missed the connection, but that was an outlier). I paid the default £6 and settled into a window seat to trundle along to St Ives via Hayle. 40 minutes later, the bus arrived in town, did a funky turn-around move in an area just outside the train station which was most definitely *not* suited for double decker bus manoeuvres, and stopped at the side of the road to let us all get off.

It was a little after 10am, and I'd planned to be on the path out of St Ives to Zennor by 11am, so I wasn't in a rush. I wandered around aimlessly for a bit, enjoying for a moment the lack of (self-imposed) time pressure and just looked at the harbour. I watched a gutsy, massive seagull nick bits of what I assume was fish scraps out of a big, deep plastic box. Which reminded me that I ought to get some food, so googled some options and headed to Norway Stores up the road. It was a small shop with high-end food, not really ideal for on-the-road hiking snacks, but after some pondering, I grabbed a pack of prosciutto, a bag of Kettle Chips and a couple of fresh croissants.

I walked a little more around town, heading out to St Ives Head and looking around at the coast guard station. I noticed the coastguard get into a nice red Tesla Model 3 parked next to the building, nice choice! I then followed Standard Operating Procedure and got lost down a path, u-turned and followed the correct route past the Tate Gallery, Porthmeor beach and on to Man's Head out of town on the infamous "tough section" at just around 11am as planned.

It started off easy - it was just a tarmac path. A bit boring really, to the point where I wondered why so far along it was *still* a tarmac path. A few hundred metres later around Clodgy Point, the path turned back to a track cut in the ground, and a little further along I was on a set of large stepping stones. In winter, this area would be boggy and partially under water, but in September after a fair period of good weather the ground was dry, making the going fairly easy. A runner came up behind me and I stepped in to let him pass, momentarily envious of the speed he was travelling at with no pack. He had headphones in, so I didn't try to start a conversation.

As I went on, it became apparent that the path is not so much brutal, as brutally annoying. Rather than totally flat or gravelly ground, the route is mostly light, loose stone or packed earth but has lots of irregular granite rocks sticking up, meaning you have to concentrate on every step to ensure you don't trip, although the confidence attained by using walking poles did let me relax a bit more as I could catch all but the worst of trips using my arms. Periodically, there were stacks of boulders to negotiate - some no worse than a style while others required a bit of clambering around on hands and feet to safely get back to ground level. None were dangerous or difficult, and on the whole the climbing around was actually quite fun, but all these things transpire to slow you down and sap energy. And no section is really flat. You're always going a little uphill or a little downhill, nothing major, but combined with everything else it's just difficult to get a rhythm on that section.

I caught up with a man and his two young daughters who were walking well, the girls who must have been at most 10 years old skipping over the rocks and making light work of the path. We talked, and I found out they were doing the full section to Pendeen and I said how impressed I was that the girls were happy to do all that distance! They lived fairly locally so knew the terrain and it was their local stomping ground, and getting on to the subject of running we discussed some of the races in the area too.

A little later, the same runner I had passed earlier had stopped and was looking at maps on his phone. He asked if there was a cut-through to the road from here, but as far as I know the only real exit points from the path in this section are St Ives and Zennor. I did point out that a guy that I was recently chatting to behind us knew the area better than I did so it would be worth going back and asking him, and off he went.

Around 12pm, somewhere near Economy Cove and a little way before Zennor Head, I did something I had rarely done up to now - I took my pack off and sat down. I wasn't really physically tired; I just wanted a bit of a mental break for 5 minutes. I sat down and had croissants and prosciutto, and just spent a few minutes taking in the view. And what a view it was. Rough landscape, multiple headlands in either direction, with Zennor Head prominent to the west and rocks jutting out near the coast and then poking up again further out to sea.

The rocks on the path got bigger and more frequent, the hills a little steeper and longer and an hour later I was on Zennor Head looking down towards Pendour Cove set in the beautiful mineral turquoise sea.

I had been walking up and down narrow paths, some wet where the path was also a stream flowing down from the land above, when I met an older lady walking down towards me. She had an old coat and one walking pole, and was carefully but confidently coming down a fairly technical section. She was a lovely lady - she lived locally, was retired, rode her horse and got out for a walk of a mile or two every single day on the path despite being the best part of 70. Her knees were a bit shot, hence the walking pole, but come rain or shine, she'd be out there - nothing was going to stop her daily walk!

Another hour of much the same terrain, and Pendeen cliffs were visible in the far distance although at this point I couldn't make out the Pendeen Watch lighthouse with my rubbish eyes. It hadn't been a long day so far with my late start, but I was getting a little tired. The view - whilst amazing - was very similar as you reappeared from each climb, or rounded each corner, with Pendeen in the distance, teasing me but not appearing to get any closer.

Porthmeor Cove was a particular highlight, another beautiful rocky cove set into the rocks, for just me to enjoy with no one else about at all.

I caught up with a couple who were walking to Pendeen from Zennor, and we chatted about the path. Like many other walkers, they were doing the path in sections, taking it slowly and really enjoying today. It was nice talking to people who were having a great time and loving the atmosphere of the path. I always came away smiling after saying goodbye when chatting with positive people.

Eventually, around 4 hours after starting on this section of path, I could make out Pendeen Watch lighthouse. I dropped down at Portheras Cove and crossed a little wooden bridge over a clear, fast flowing stream. I thought I'd take the opportunity to fill up my water bottles, so I dropped my pack down and got out my squeezy water filter. Dunking the pouch under the water of the stream, I then squeezed it through the filter to completely fill my bottles with clean, clear, hopefully virus and bacteria-free water. While I was doing this, the couple I'd previously passed

169

walked by and commented on how useful the filter looked as they'd not seen one before.

Moving on from Portheras Cove I arrived at Pendeen Watch lighthouse at almost exactly 4 o'clock. It had taken me 5 hours to do the 13 miles from St Ives to Pendeen.

Pendeen evokes bittersweet memories for me. In 2017, I visited for the first time to look around as part of my recce for the Arc of Attrition before doing it for the first time early the following year. I didn't go far as I'd had my appendix whipped out about 3 weeks earlier and I wasn't supposed to be running at all, let alone scouting a few miles along the coast path, so it was leisurely, with the family and both exciting and enjoyable.

In 2018, my cousin Culvin ran the whole of the coast path in 22 days spread over a few months, and I joined him for a couple of days from Portreath through to Lamorna, which included this section on the first day. It was a long day, and we got to Pendeen at sunset. Add in the relief of nearly being at our accommodation for the day and that was both a beautiful and emotional place.

Skip on another year or so, and at the end of January 2019 I arrived at Pendeen coming up from Land's End at about 5am, having left a snowy Coverack 17 hours and 70 miles earlier. It was raining, about 4°C and I was doing a pretty good impression of Herr Flick from 'Allo 'Allo! (now *there's* a reference from the 80's). I couldn't bend my right leg, and hadn't been able to for the best part of the last 15 miles, diagnosed by the physio at Land's End as suffering from knee bursitis. I was having such a good time I didn't want to stop. But here the legendary status of the Pendeen to St Ives section combined with my basic inability to go up hills, or down hills, or to really move very well even on the flat meant this was the end point - to date the furthest I've got in that race.

So now, for the fourth time, I was at Pendeen. This time, there was no sunset, no knackered knee (thankfully!) and no major emotion. It was just a lighthouse, and I was pleased to get past it, focussed on the next few miles and getting to my destination.

One problem with hitting Pendeen at 5am in January is that you can't see much, so my 2019 experience of the place didn't reveal too much detail for the section south. But when I passed through with Culvin in 2018 on the morning of our second day I remember it being the moment that I fell in love with the Cornish mine country.

Past Pendeen Watch lighthouse, you continue up a stretch of road, then off to a path on the right and down into a not too steep valley, cross a small stream and back up the other side, at which point you pop over the hill to see Geevor Tin Mine in the distance.

Geevor tin mine (*Whel an Gever* in Cornish, or "mine of the goats") was in operation from 1911 thorough to 1990, making it almost the last tin mine in operation in Cornwall (that accolade goes to South Crofty which closed in 1998). During it's time it produced 50,000 tons of black tin from around 85 miles of underground tunnels - let that sink in for a minute... that's a *lot* of tunnels. Since 1992, after its closure, Geevor has been the site of a mining and heritage centre and at 67 acres is the largest preserved mining site in Great Britain. Each time I've passed through I've been on another mission, so I've never visited the mining museum but it was highly recommended by a chap wearing a hard hat that I spoke to on the way through this time and it's definitely on my to-do list when I return. Which I will, without a shadow of a doubt.

A little further on, looking back and down to the sea level was the famous Crown engine houses of Botallack mine. Under this innocuous looking building, tunnels extend up to half a mile under the sea and down as far as 550m. Over its life from sometime in the 18th century through to 1895, the mine extracted an estimated 14,500 tonnes of tin, 20,000 tonnes of copper and 1,500 tonnes of arsenic, along with around 1.5 *million* tonnes of waste!

Interestingly, while chatting to Howard walking yesterday, he mentioned that there is talk of various mines in Cornwall potentially reopening. The growth of various electronic industries has caused the demand for various raw materials like tin and arsenic to skyrocketed. With product scarcity driving up prices, it's looking like it may become economical once again to run mining operations in Cornwall.

My feet crunched the ground, my poles clacked on the rocks and I continued on the path. And then, in the distance, I spied the headland of Cape Cornwall with its distinctive chimney on top.

If I had to pick "a favourite place in the world", it would be Cape Cornwall. I'm not entirely sure why. It's a combination of intense memories, the general atmosphere of the place and the immense history of the whole area, but also the fact that every time I've been there - day or night - it's never been too busy. You can actually stop for a minute and just *appreciate* the place in your own personal space.

Part of the Cape Cornwall Mine, the prominent chimney dates back to 1864. The mine operated between 1838 and 1883, after which it was closed permanently and although the engine house was demolished, the chimney was retained for navigation purposes. Until the early 19th century when the first Ordnance Survey was completed, it was believed to be the most westerly point in Cornwall.

From the point where it was first visible, it took a while to get to Cape Cornwall. The path undulates a little and winds around the Kenidjack Valley so it's not a direct route, but after a while you come down beside the road towards the Cape Cornwall headland.

As I write this and looking back at the tracks my watch recorded, I realise I went a bit wrong here. Once I got near the main car park, I went through a gate onto the road and on to what I knew was the coast path heading south out of Cape Cornwall. What I've only just realised from looking at my watch track and the maps is that the coast path actually runs a little further west, over the headland and past the chimney, then down and back inland to meet the route I took. Although it would have been a bit of extra climbing, I'm sad to have got this wrong - I would have loved to go up past the chimney but I was probably

173

a bit too intent on getting to the end of the day and thought I knew the route (big mistake!) so missed the sign for the correct route.

The plan for the day had me ending just after Cape Cornwall around Cot Valley, and the youth hostel was only a short way from here, or at least it looked like it on the map. I passed the turn for the SWCP, ignored it and carried on inland up the valley, updating my GPS to guide me to the hostel. I turned down a road, over a bridge, into a small alley beside a building and was starting to get a bit worried that I was on a wild goose chase instigated by my GPS when I spotted a YHA sign, headed up some steps and there it was.

I've never been to a youth hostel before and wasn't quite sure what to expect. It was an attractive looking, big white building with a gravel car park. The main door was open so I went in. The guy at the reception checked me in, told me about the camping area out the back of the building, the shower block for campers, and about the available food and - most importantly - beer options. Sorted!

There were residents in the main building but no one else was camping, so I had the whole garden area to myself - nice and flat, with a fantastic view down the valley to the sea. It was about 6pm, sunset wasn't for another couple of hours so I could leisurely set up the tent. I was definitely getting better at it: a perfect tent set up first time, nice and taught, all the extra lines in place, plenty of headroom inside the tent and with the open door facing the view.

I'm not entirely sure what was upstairs in the hostel - I assume rooms and bathrooms - but downstairs there was a big dining area so I went in to see what I could get. The food options were… pizza. And that was absolutely fine by me. I ordered a chicken and bacon pizza and a bottle of Porthleven.

Side note now: At the time I had no idea what Porthleven beer was like, but I *did* know the place it was named after. Round about 25 miles from Coverack, 15 from the Lizard and about 15 from Penzance, Porthleven is the first aid station on the Arc of Attrition. Arriving between 5 and 6pm (after starting from Coverack at 12pm), it's a welcome spot for fuelling up with coffee and hot food before committing to head torches for the next 12 or 13 hours enroute to Porthtowan.

It turns out at this youth hotel that the guy who checked me in (who I *think* was called Richard… we'll go with that), was also the guy who… well, basically did everything. I ordered my pizza through the hatch with him, and got my drink from him, and then my food was delivered to my table 15 minutes later by him as well. He was great as a hotel receptionist, spot on as a barman, and perfect as a chef and waiter. So, thank you Richard (if that's your name) - very much appreciated!

There were 4 sets of people in the dining room, 3 of us on our own and one couple. The couple were the only ones initially talking, and it was a bit of an odd conversation. From what I overheard, I think they'd been to a wedding and the woman was unimpressed by a lot of it, while the man was just quietly agreeing. Then she started trying to get him to guess the grape

175

variety for the quarter-bottle of cheap wine they had ordered, getting him to "sniff the bouquet". They seemed a bit pretentious for a youth hostel I must admit, but maybe my expectation was wrong? The other 2 people were initially working, one on a computer and the other writing notes in a book. We got chatting a little later, and the one on the computer turned out to be a Youth Hostel Association inspector who was doing rounds and checking safety at the sites. The other lady was walking the whole coast path over a good number of years, enjoying herself and writing copious notes about her experiences. I had the usual slightly awkward conversation about how far I'd gone each day, and how impressive it was.

On that note, it would be wrong to say part of me didn't love the surprise people showed when you tell them you've done 38 miles in a day with a big pack on, and 200-odd miles in the last week. But mostly, I felt a bit embarrassed - like I was trying to show off - which absolutely wasn't the intention. I enjoy the challenge of trying to move fast, and I love the landscape of the South West Coast Path. But for me, I didn't feel like I was going all that quickly. I spend a lot of my time mixing with various people who cover 26 miles in under 2 hours 30 minutes, 100km (62 miles) in well under 7 hours and 160 miles in 24 hours. And spending too much time reading about the likes of Damian Hall, who amongst many other great achievements, covered the whole coast path in 10 days and a few hours.

To me, I wasn't going particularly quickly at all. But if I take a mental step back, I know I was probably covering distances faster than about 95% of anyone else doing the coast path. It's funny how your perception of normality is so influenced by the people you surround yourself with.

I don't remember exactly but I think I may have snuck in another Porthleven (and I'm conscious of sounding like an alcoholic on this trip, but it's all calories!), then paid up and went back to my tent to get bottles and my head torch as it was almost dark at this point. I then went back inside for some water for the night time. I always like to have a bottle of water in the tent so if I wake up thirsty, I can sort it out there and then, rather than starting the day needing water. This could potentially lead to the terrible issue of needing to get out the tent for the toilet in the middle of the night, but I figured that the risk was worth it!

Anyway, with my head torch on my head (where else would it be?) I headed back to the building to ask if they could fill my water bottles. As I made my way to the dining room, I was met by Richard along with the lady who was inspecting the youth hostels for safety. She made the point that I was well prepared and had a head torch on, and it turns out at that moment they were discussing the lighting around the building to make sure that there was enough and it was safe, and I was being used as an edge-case of someone who was prepared in their own way! After a laugh about this situation, I asked if they could fill my water bottles up. As I mentioned before, I'm really not all that familiar with youth hostels, and they both pointed out that there's a self-catering kitchen next door to the dining room which made me feel a tad silly. It was a jolly nice kitchen too, and again, I can highly recommend a stay at Land's End YHA hostel whether you want food cooked for you, or you have a cookable feast in your pack needing no more than 2 ovens, 8 hobs and a microwave.

Back under canvas, I settled down for my last night in a tent, with only 1 more day to walk tomorrow. On my mat, covered in my sleeping bag, I fiddled on my phone and found the perfect podcast to listen to tonight - *Mark Steel's in Town* all about Penzance, where I was heading tomorrow. I laughed a lot in the tent that night, in particular about the passage from the Cornish Survival Guide:

"Folks still seem to think we Cornish is primitive, smugglers, a bit dangerous. But these days yous more likely to have your ear talked off than hacked off with a rusty cutlass" And then it says "Note. This don't apply to St Just"

It's lucky I'm not in a tent... spitting distance from St Just!

I'm not sure if that had really dawned on me at that point. As I sit and write this a good few weeks after I finished the walk, I look back at these key times - the last night in a tent being an example - and think they should have been more poignant. But hindsight and rose-tinted glasses put a different perspective on all memories. If I'm being honest, I think I was just glad of another safe, secure night, in my canvas bag that I was getting more and more familiar and comfortable with, falling asleep listening to a podcast about maths or science or some comedy or other and knowing that tomorrow I'd be repeating the same thing as today. It had been going for enough days for it to become a pattern. A habit. A normality. I think maybe just as I was about to finish, I'd actually settled into the whole thing.

CHAPTER 11

Day 9: St Just to Penzance

"They think it's all over. It is now."

- Kenneth Wolstenholme

Start Time	**8:07am**
Total Distance	**22.06 miles**
Elevation	**4044 feet**
Total Time	**7 hours 26 mins**
Moving Time	**5 hours 59 mins (16:17mins/mile)**
Steps	**45143**

I tossed and turned a little during my sleep, and in the middle of the night I lay awake for enough time to know I was lying awake wondering if I'd get back to a good sleep, but then I fell asleep for long enough to have a good sleep. All of that is a complicated way of saying that I basically had a pretty solid, refreshing sleep.

Which got me thinking... (oh no, here I go again) What *is* a good sleep? Before I left on my adventure, it was a good, solid 8-or-so hours. In a comfy bed. With a pillow, and a duvet, and heating and all the normal stuff you get used to in this day and age in our part of the world. But after 8 nights on the path, my needs - or rather my perception of my needs - had changed. It was difficult to describe what made a good night's sleep, because I'd had everything from fairly solid sleep to almost no sleep at all. And yet (almost) every day I'd managed to do what needed to be done, without feeling what I'd describe as *tired*. And for me, that was a big deal.

In my normal not-walking-on-the-coast-path life, I often use the fact that "I'm tired" as an excuse for anything and everything. It's why my work didn't go well today. Why I'm grumpy. Why I don't want to go for a run. I *know* I only had 7 hours of sleep last night instead of 8, and that's what's causing all my problems today. But after these days of, well, basically pretty crap sleeping in a tent, I know that's rubbish.

You can cope with what you need to cope with, as long as you have something above a minimum amount of sleep. That's going

181

to depend on each person, but I'll take a fair bet that it's a LONG way down on what you *think* you need. It certainly is for me, and there's one of many unexpected but concrete lessons from this experience. I'm not good at learning by being *told*, I tend to learn best when I'm *shown*, so hopefully this one will stick with me!

Early on in this adventure, I hit a low point. I hadn't had much sleep, but I'm not sure if I hadn't had *enough*. I certainly got low - low enough to reconsider the whole endeavour, to question why the hell I was doing it at all, or certainly in the intense way I was doing it. But in hindsight - that oh so wonderful of things - I think a single multi-day test would have woken me up to the low that could happen... and how easy it was to fix. It comes down to the absolute basics - all I really needed was some promise of shelter and food occasionally. It didn't have to be every night, just every few nights. I could survive one crap night, even two or three. But not an indefinite, unknown amount. I think the fear of what *might* happen was by far the biggest thing to mess with my head.

That got a bit deep! Especially as I had what I can only really describe as a decent night sleep on that night in my tent just outside St Just, setting me up well for my last day of walking.

The distance wasn't too long today, similar to yesterday at a bit over 20 miles so my alarm was set for 7am. The early morning gently lit the inside of the tent and I woke gently and naturally about 15 minutes before the alarm. It was another morning of light rain outside, again sounding louder on the tent than you would expect for the amount of the actual rain. I did a fair amount of packing and changing inside the tent before opening the front up and seeing the grey skies, clouds and the great view down to the sea.

Eva had booked my pitch, and along with it had added the breakfast option of a bap so after a quick wash I headed inside at 7:30am and got a cup of strong black wake-up-juice and a sausage bap from the omnipresent Richard. It was the first time I'd had something warm before I'd even put the tent away, and I enjoyed it very much. It felt leisurely, civilised and I could just relax and take my time easing into the day.

Back outside, the rain had stopped so I dragged everything outside on my plastic sheet and packed the tent away for the final time. At just after 8am, I said goodbye to Richard, thanked him for a great stay, then headed off back down the steps, down the alleyway, round the corner, onto the road and back down to the SWCP marker I'd walked past yesterday evening.

The weather was dull and grey with a bit of a breeze and the hint of rain in the air. It wasn't actually raining, but it felt like it could at any time. It was warm though, and I was plenty warm enough with just my t-shirt on so I didn't bother with my coat.

The landscape was just stunning. A mix of green, brown, purple and yellow fern, heather and grass coated the granite, with various exposed sections of orange rocks cutting into the hills. Granite cliffs fell away into the sea, then rose back up in jutting rocks as they went further out from the land. The whole place glowed with colour against the grey sky.

Ten minutes after leaving the youth hostel I was rising up on the other side of the Cot Valley, looking down at the car park at Porth Nanven. I remember reading news reports of a man who had fallen down a mineshaft here back in 2017. He fell more than 15 metres into the shaft, and suffering from hypothermia and broken bones was eventually rescued after 5 hours by a team of more than 50 people. He was lucky, and it shows how relatively easy it is to end up in trouble in this landscape... and how difficult it could be to get back out again. It's worth treating Cornish mining country with great respect, those mines may be hidden in the countryside now but they have teeth and bite if you're not careful, which just adds to the mystique, intrigue and appeal as far as I'm concerned. In a world where Health & Safety applies to everything, a thousand random, hidden, deep shafts in the countryside forces you to take a bit of responsibility for yourself.

Rounding the corner, I could see Sennen Cove. In the distance was Longships lighthouse, built on Carn Bras, the tallest of the Longships islets and situated just over a mile off the western-most point of mainland England. As I continued southwards and gained some altitude on the green, yellow and purple hills, the buildings of Sennen became clearer and I looked back with a tinge of sadness for a last glimpse of Cape Cornwall before it disappeared around the headland. I'd definitely be back, but it might be a while before I was.

The path was fairly easy to move along, although there were plenty of jutting rocks to keep you concentrating. At a few points, the granite of the cliffs formed big boulders covering the path and it was quite fun to climb up and down these, which was lucky because there was no other way to get past them!

Just around Aire Point at the northern end of Whitesand Bay, the golden stretch of Gwynver beach was visible in the distance along the great brown and grey boulder-strewn curve of the coastline. Out to sea, there were a few people wind foiling (or wing foiling? I'm not too clear on the differences - they were on boards holding wings anyway). The path went along the back of the beach, on sand and through dunes then inland a little behind Sennen beach. Narrowing to a path lined with hedges that I remembered running along in the other direction in the dark with a head torch some years before, I went down into the car park at Sennen Cove. Walking along past the shops, this was the first real bit of civilisation on the path since St Ives.

An hour and a half after leaving the hostel, I was climbing steps on the path out of Sennen Cove just a mile or so from Land's End. And just before 10am, I was at the western most point in England. I had to check the exact description, and it is specifically *England* - there's a place in the Scottish Highlands called Corrachadh Mòr which is fractionally further west, making that the western most point in mainland Great Britain.

It has to be said - I'm not a big fan of Land's End. I mean, I love the landscape, and I love the general area, but I don't like the commercialisation: big white buildings, huge car parks, railings, signs, and the various big bright coloured posters to suck in the tourists. At 10am on a grey Monday morning in mid-

September there weren't many people, but that almost made it worse. It gave the place a derelict feel, like today there was no purpose at all for the existence of the buildings.

I wasn't really hungry, but I thought I probably ought to get some food given the opportunity and there was a big glass door in a big white building so I went through it. Inside was a pretty decent looking buffet and a waitress walked by carrying a tray of fried eggs - this was looking good! She stopped to ask me if I was here for breakfast. Having looked around at people sitting at tables, none of whom had outdoor clothes on, it now dawned on me that I had wandered into the restaurant of a hotel and sadly this fine spread was for the residents only, not the smelly, muddy outdoor type that had just wandered in! She clarified this for me, and I headed back out the door I came in, empty handed. The waitress had mentioned that the cafe would be open either at 10 or 10:30am, but I was now in a grump and decided not to give any custom to the area. This didn't improve my view of Land's End - give me Cape Cornwall any day.

As I walked around the building to get back on the path, I passed the famous sign post with distances to John O Groats, New York and so on, where you can have your picture taken. Immediately, I thought of Mark Steel's comments on his podcast that I listened to in the tent last night:

"And when they leave, they lock the sign post away. I have to admire that as what is, undoubtedly, the most mean-spirited tourist attraction in the whole country!"

186

A concrete block with a white post poking up into the air stood against the sea and sky. Lying half hidden on the floor against the back wall was the fingerpost with the distances to John O Groats and New York. I took a picture of the "post with no sign", chuckled at the memory of that podcast last night, then headed off away from the commercialisation of the landscape back into mother nature at around 10am.

As I hadn't managed to score a plate of delicious breakfast, I reached round into the top of my back to see what nibbles I could find. I happened across a block of Kendal Mint Cake that Eva had bought me to bring on this trip when we were in Dartmoor a few weeks back, and snapped a few chunks off. I'm not sure I've ever had mint cake, but this was absolutely delicious! It was almost pure sugar so I wasn't sure how long it would keep me going before I succumbed to some sort of crash, but it tasted lovely.

On past Land's End, the landscape still had the granite rocks and cliffs. There was more heather and grass, giving the area a predominantly green and brown tint and making it feel less rough, less raw than the northern coast. There were more signs of people around here too - occasional but continuous houses and buildings on the hills in the distance. There were lots of little coves with epic granite cliffs looking like they'd been smashed out of the ground by a giant.

The rain started getting heavier and more persistent, although still not quite enough to warrant stopping and putting my coat on. I thought there was much more chance of cooking myself if I put my coat on than of any issues from getting a bit wet, especially with it being my last day and not having quite such a need to avoid the sort of issues you might get from wet clothes, like chafing.

But combined with the wind, the rain did serve to dampen the mood a bit. I should have been enjoying this section, but I wasn't really. On reflection, I think my mind had gotten into an "I'm nearly there" mindset and everything between now and the end was just something to overcome, something to get through as quickly as possible and I wasn't really taking in the beauty or uniqueness of the landscape.

Human brains are wired to react to change, and they settle when enough time has passed that the change becomes normality. Take the example of travelling from an English town to a Swiss mountain resort (bear with me…) On the first morning, you open the curtains and are astounded by the view, spending a long time just taking in the beauty of this new and unfamiliar environment. A week later, having seen it for hours and hours during the days, you open the curtains and barely notice the mountains. I think I was getting a bit like that on the path, which was both a good and a bad thing. It was a good thing as - had I been continuing - my mind and body were getting thoroughly used to the continual daily challenges. But it was bad as I wasn't fully appreciating the stunning beauty, the cliffs, the landscape, and the history of the place. And this was accentuated by me almost being at the end. I felt a little like I was deliberately trying not to enjoy it as I was about to stop, as a sort-of protection mechanism to stop me being too upset about ending early.

At Porthgwarra I passed a little beach cafe hut but wasn't really interested in getting any food or drink so didn't stop. I took a look down to the beach and there was an interesting tunnel in the rocks, cut by tin miners from St Just almost 150 years ago to give farmers access to the beach via horse and cart so they could collect seaweed to use as a fertiliser.

Up the hill out of Porthgwarra, looking back you could no longer see any hint of Land's End, and 20 minutes later I was in Porthcurno, in a car park, looking down towards the beautiful beach.

There's some great history associated with Porthcurno. On Minack Point lies the famous Minack Theatre - a unique open-air theatre, built almost single-handedly by Rowena Cade, who moved to Cornwall after the first world war. In the early 1930s, local village players had staged Shakespeare's *The Tempest* in a roughly constructed theatre in her garden against the backdrop of the sea, and the play was such a success she resolved to improve the theatre. She worked into her 80's, through the winters with the area being used for plays in the summer. Despite having visited the car park on 4 occasions now, I've never actually seen the theatre itself… another thing to add to the to-do list.

There is also a big history of telecommunications in Porthcurno. In 1870, the beach became the termination point of one of the first submarine telegraph cables linking the UK to India. In the early 20th century, the cable office operated as many as 14 cables making it, for a short time, the largest submarine cable station in the world. The cable office closed in 1970, but the engineering college remained open until the 1990s, training apprentices in telecommunications. Many important submarine cables still run into Porthcurno, but now they connect to the national communications network, running through wires under the road and popping out in Skewjack a few miles inland from Porthcurno.

To get to the beach, you have to go down a set of steep, uneven steps cut into the side of the cliff face. I'm a little familiar with these, having climbed them twice around midnight on winter nights, but now I could see them in the full light of day I was nervous descending, especially with a heavy pack on my back. I don't think there's much danger of falling off the cliff, but it can feel like it as you're carefully taking each step at a time on some sections.

I passed around the back of the beach, spotting the small hut just down towards the sea from the path. This inconspicuous building was built in 1929 and is where all the telegraph cables actually came ashore. Should you choose, you can look through the door and see cables snaking up from the ground, the largest collection of original historical telegraph cables and connection boxes in the world.

I remember having an amazing time around here in that second year of running the Arc race back in 2018, middle of the night, headtorch blazing, having just almost skipped my way down the steep hill that now stood ahead of me. But now, on this blustery September day I wasn't looking forward to the next section. I was ready to be finished. At around 11:30am, I headed up the hill out of Porthcurno without even stopping to look into the cable station hut.

Twenty minutes later I walked through Penberth Cove, a tiny, beautiful fishing village, and in another 45 minutes the path met St Loy's cove. Here, you have to walk across the beach, balancing on top of the boulders that cover the coast. From previous experience I was expecting slow progress across the boulders, but I'd never tried it with walking poles before and quickly found I could more or less skip across them with the extra support from the poles. It only took a few minutes, but by the end I was bouncing between rocks with a big smile on my face, not wanting to get back on to the solid ground.

When I walked this section with Culvin back in 2018, we were both getting tired towards the end of the second day and I remember being teased by a white lighthouse in the distance that seemed to not get any closer even after what felt like hours of walking towards it. This time round, I kept looking out for that lighthouse but couldn't see it at all. I started to wonder if I'd been misremembering, when suddenly I passed a gate at the top of a slope and at the bottom there it was - Tater-du Lighthouse. I hadn't gone (completely) mad, but I still don't quite understand why it had been so visible in 2018 and yet despite looking out for it, I'd not seen it until literally on top of it this time round. As I found out later, on the rocks below the lighthouse the upturned wreck of the *Union Star* was found on the 20th December 1981, 16 people having lost their lives in the stormy seas of the previous night.

I knew I couldn't be too far from Lamorna Cove now, and that little harbour has a special place in my heart. Back in 2007, we stayed in a little house called Pirate's Cottage in Penzance for a week over Christmas, and I remember coming here a little after sunset whilst out on a drive visiting places in the local area. Having driven down a particularly windy, narrow Cornish coast road, we had stood in the car park soaking up the late evening atmosphere and looking out to sea, watching a solitary seal bobbing up and down. It's always been known as "Seal Cove" to us from that time.

In 2017, while on my fact-finding recce before I ran the Arc for the first time, as well as Pendeen we also came down here and in my post-appendectomy state I carefully went half a mile or so along the path east towards Mousehole. I tried to go along the path on the other side - towards Land's End - but couldn't get far as it involved climbing (which I wasn't supposed to be doing) over some quite big boulders on the edge of a drop into the sea that was big enough to give you some serious problems if you fell off it! After that - and until I actually got to this point during the Arc in 2019 - I was quite concerned about that section at night, imagining being petrified by the drops while clambering over boulders with nothing but the light of my head torch. But when I finally did get there at around 11pm on a cool, windy January night in 2019, I absolutely *loved* it!

And now here I was, coming at it from Land's End, over those boulders by that drop into the sea, not concerned about falling off at all, but hoping that round the corner I'd be able to get a cup of coffee and something to eat.

And, thankfully, there was. After getting over the climbs, not falling in the sea and then walking a little distance on some flat ground, a whole set of outside tables and chairs and a cafe came into view around the corner as I got into Lamorna Cove. I went into the cafe and ordered a Cornish pasty along with my usual black americano from the possibly most bored, uninterested girl in the world (although she was a teenager, and in my experience that's pretty much their default state). With the order safely in the system somewhere I proffered my phone for a card payment. "Cash is preferred," she said in a robotic, monotonous voice, like she was repeating the phrase for the millionth time. In 2021, with the world changed after Covid, it was generally unusual for respectable establishments to want cash payment in place of a card. I must have looked as exasperated as I felt when I dumped my bag down and started digging through for cash that she said that she could accept a card payment if she absolutely *had* to, so I took her up on the offer without feeling remotely bad about it and paid with my phone.

At 1:30pm, I was sitting on a bench with a very, very hot black americano and a very hot Cornish pasty which, once cooled, was delicious! I was looking out to sea from the harbour and remembering that night in December when, as a family, we were watching that seal bobbing about in the dark waters.

According to the calculations on The Plan, Lamorna to Mousehole was around 2.5 miles. Coming in the other direction and at night, I remembered there being a section of road that dropped down a slope to go alongside the sea, and I thought that was between Lamorna and Mousehole so I was thinking that there must only be at most another 1½ miles of path to go before I was off any uneven path and on the road for the final stretch. This pleased me.

I had been getting progressively more fed up with the path. Large sections were quite overgrown, making using the poles difficult and I was constantly running into bushes or catching my feet on roots. And there were bees and wasps - the former I'm fairly happy with, but I've got a bit of an irrational fear of wasps so I was tense pushing my way along some of the buzzier sections. The higher vegetation either side of the path meant the view was limited too, and rather than being faced with great vistas of rock, cliffs and sea I spent much more time looking down a tunnel of bushes.

After pasty munching, and waiting for the coffee to cool down from a temperature that would strip skin from bones to merely scalding hot, I sipped it down then got up to leave. When I went to pick up my poles, I noticed a definite lack of any poles. I'd read about other people walking the path and leaving walking poles on boats, busses and various other places, but figured I wouldn't make that sort of mistake... no, not me. Turns out I was wrong. So I went back into the cafe, hoping I'd left them in there. One advantage of having bright red-and-yellow poles is that they're difficult to lose, so they were pretty obvious to spot against the wall by the counter.

Out of Lamorna, the path wound up the hill with overhanging trees, feeling like a forest glade. There were some granite boulders and it was quite enjoyable although I was beginning to get a bit physically tired now and I was feeling it in my legs as I clambered up and over with my pack. A little way further along, I climbed up some rocks that felt almost like I was climbing up a small waterfall as a stream ran down getting my feet quite wet. I then entered a wooded section that I remembered from past experience at night as somewhere that was a bit confusing, but I figured with it being daylight it would be obvious where to go.

I crouched down to slide under a fallen tree (which was no mean feat with a hefty pack on my back) and came up in a clearing. There was an old brick wall at one side, and more huge fallen trees and roots in every direction, with no obvious path to follow. As I was looking around, a lady I had passed a little earlier came into the same area, so together we climbed around looking for the way out. It had to be around somewhere, but there was nothing obvious.

I retraced my steps back under the fallen tree to where I'd entered the clearing, and there, pretty much ahead of me but slightly off to one side and quite hidden was a gap in the trees. Heading through, I could see a path forming from the woodland into the distance, and I called back with some relief to say I'd found the way. Carrying on up the hill, it soon turned into a road.

So that was it.

I knew I had no more coastal path. No more woodlands. No more granite rocks to climb or avoid tripping over. No more mines or engine houses. No more woodland or trees. It was just road and pavement to the end now. And at that very point in time, I was quite happy about that.

My phone rang. That hadn't happened for a while, but I was expecting a call. My son was on the other end. "Well?", I said.

"I passed, with 1 minor!", came the reply. Fantastic news - after many delays and cancellation due to the pandemic, the roads now had another driver! I congratulated him and chatted away on the phone just as my road-legs came into play and I picked up speed on the ascent past some people out for a wander. The news had really lifted my spirits.

Down into Mousehole (pronounced "muzzle") harbour, I took a couple of photos on my phone, then tried to style-out having gone completely the wrong way. It would have worked if I didn't then go completely the wrong way again down a dead end. And again. I really am bloody awful at navigation!

Eventually I escaped from Mousehole along the characteristically narrow roads which were full of traffic. Such a quaint and beautiful place attracts a lot of people, 99% of whom try to get there by car so they don't have to walk more than 6 feet to see what all the fuss is about. Then they get out of their car and complain about all the cars around. The ridiculous traffic detracts so much from the inherent beauty of the place, an insoluble conundrum as the thin streets are both key to the historical feeling and the very reason why it's not suitable for a mass of tourists descending on the place.

I thought there was a memorial in Mousehole to the lifeboat disaster that happened nearby in 1981, and had a brief look around but couldn't see anything so carried on along the route to Newlyn on the outskirts of Penzance.

10 minutes later I passed the now disused Penlee lifeboat station and the memorial I had been looking for.

In December 1981, the *Union Star* left Holland on her maiden voyage to Ireland with a crew of 4 as well as Captain Henry Morton, his wife and two teenage stepdaughters who they picked up enroute so they could all be together for the holidays. At 6pm on 19th December 1981, Falmouth Coastguard received a distress call from the coaster - their engines had stopped and would not restart. Rough seas and heavy winds were blowing the vessel towards the treacherous Cornish cliffs. The lifeboat *Solomon Browne* was put on standby.

With one fuel tank filled with water, starting the engines aboard the *Union Star* was impossible. The first rescue attempts were made by an RNAS Sea King helicopter, but the pitching and rolling of the ship in the storm seas was so violent that the mast threatened to collide with the helicopter. The airborne rescue mission was called off and switched to sea with the launch of the lifeboat into hurricane force 12 gales - 90 knot winds and

18-metre-high waves - to rescue those on board the stricken vessel that was now less than 2 miles away from the coast of Cornwall.

The lifeboat fought for half an hour to get alongside the *Union Star*, with the helicopter above, unable to help but keeping watch on how things were going. From his position in the air, Lieutenant Commander Russell Smith saw dark shapes and fluorescent jackets moving around on the deck back towards the lifeboat.

The lifeboat crew managed to rescue 4 of the 8 people from the ship and radio this to the coast guard, at which point the helicopter turned back to shore assuming the lifeboat would head back to shore. But the crew made one final heroic rescue attempt.

All radio contact was lost.

The next day, the *Union Star* was found capsized by the rocks of Tater Du lighthouse, and the wreckage of the lifeboat began to wash ashore. All 8 people on board the *Union Star* and the full crew of 8 on the lifeboat were lost that day.

I stood for a while, reading the wording on the memorial and just thinking about what it must have been like. 8pm in December, pitch black, howling hurricane winds and crashing seas. Eight people make the decision to go out in those conditions to rescue another 8 people. What absolute heroes those men were. A very sobering moment.

Ten minutes later I'm reminded that most people are just idiots. I took a photo of a sign saying "No Parking on footpath", after having just had to walk in the road to avoid 3 cars parked on the footpath next to it.

The coast path dropped off the pavement to run closer to the sea, along a cycleway and a little later up a slope back to the pavement. *Here* was that section that I remembered earlier - I'd previously thought it was between Lamorna and Mousehole, but in fact it was just around Newlyn Harbour.

The harbour was pretty busy, there were a lot of boats of all sizes parked up (you can tell I'm a bit of an expert on all things nautical by my use of the correct terminology like *parked up*), and although with an obvious industrial air it was actually quite pretty. Once you get into the streets toward Penzance though, it's just a lot of marine related buildings, generally large and functional without much aesthetic appeal. There were a lot more people around here now too, and combined with the number of cars and still fairly narrow road sections I had to be a bit careful not to get run over. Off the more major roads, the path then turned on to the seafront and ran along the nice seafront park area of Newlyn Green.

The end of the day according to "The Plan" was at some point up the path around Marazion on the far side of Penzance, but I wasn't going all that way. Like the classy chap I am and to keep the same theme as recent days, I was heading straight for Wetherspoons to get a celebratory beer and burger. I'd looked on the map and figured I needed to turn left somewhere around Lidl and then it was more-or-less a straight line into the area of town that I needed.

I could see the big Lidl in the distance. It felt a little sad to be directing with great big white buildings on main roads rather than beautiful headlands or lighthouses in the middle of nowhere, and I just wanted to get this bit over and done with. Stomping along on concrete and tarmac for several miles was taking its toll on my feet and I was seriously looking forward to sitting down with that pint of beer.

I turned off the main road and passed a school that was just finishing, with parents and primary school children walking around the area. I'd forgotten that real-life keeps going on. I hadn't really been keeping track of what day it was, what time it was - none of that really matters when you're hiking on the path. And now, here I was, back in reality.

Further on into town, up a path that cut through the houses and across the roads, more school children of all ages walking all around. I came out of the path onto a road and followed it round to the big Lloyds Bank building in the centre of the marketplace, and there, across the street, was *The Tremenheere* where my coast path walk came to an end.

222.4 miles, 37,500ft of climbing, 8 days of walking (9 days in total including the one slacking off in the pub and on some busses).

I went through the door, and straight up to the toilets to clean up a bit. Then back down, I took a seat by the window and ordered a pint of Doom Bar. For some reason, the transaction failed, so I ordered again but ended up accidentally ordering 2 pints. Oh well, they wouldn't go to waste. I ordered a 2,000 calorie Empire State burger as well (seriously, though - unless you've just walked 200 miles, when the hell do you need a TWO THOUSAND CALORIE meal?!), and when my 2 pints arrived, I sat back and contemplated what I'd just done.

It wasn't what I'd started out to do.

It was always a long shot to do the whole path in 21 days. After the sleep issues a few days in, it had all felt so black but I was at least a little prepared for being low mentally so had promised myself not to make any rash decisions, especially early on. But it was really the logistical issues in Port Isaac that had sealed the deal. I was in a much better state of mind at that point - not sleep deprived, and generally enjoying the walking. Yet I'd still decided to end early. More thoughts on that later...

It didn't take long to drink the beer and devour the huge burger and chips. I spent some time writing a Facebook post and looking through my feed, getting unexpectedly emotional at a post by a friend who'd recently lost a much-loved collie.

After an accidental third pint (they're all accidental really, that's my excuse and I'm sticking to it!), it was late enough for me to swing my bag back onto my back and head out the door in the direction of the youth hostel on the other side of town. My watch was no longer running, so I walked the mile or two at a nice leisurely pace.

As I walked up the final section of road to the hostel, I knew I was on the right track as there was a couple in front with packs on their backs. I arrived at a considerably bigger and busier building than the Land's End hostel, queued and then checked in. My room was on the ground floor, and although the building was a bit of a maze, I found it fairly quickly.

I had the room all to myself, and it had a set of bunk beds against the wall. I don't get to sleep in a bunk bed often, so obviously I set myself up on the top one, which in hindsight may have just made things a bit more difficult having to climb up and down every time I wanted to do anything, but you've got to do these things sometimes, right?

After getting in the room, I dumped everything down, got out my "smart" clothes and wash gear and headed straight round to the shower so I could clean up. As usual, it was lovely to get out of all the sweaty gear and get cleaned up. Back in my room, I sorted a few things out in my bag so as not to have too much to do tomorrow, then went for a wander round the building to find somewhere to sit and have a beer.

Downstairs seemed to be the self-catering kitchen areas, and upstairs was accommodation so I headed back out towards the front door and found a dining area. I'd already eaten more than enough, so I got a bottle of beer (I forget which one but it wasn't a Porthleven this time) and sat to just relax somewhere other than in a bedroom on my own. There were a few people in the dining room, but all were engrossed in either phones or laptops and didn't appear up for any sort of conversation. So, I joined them, getting my phone out and flicking through some pointless social media nonsense, enjoying the fact that I didn't have to conserve battery any more.

The beer lasted longer than usual, I was nicely relaxed and just enjoying sitting there. After a while I finished, headed back to the room, had a wash at the sink in the room then climbed the ladder up into that bed in the sky.

Although not as comfortable as the bed in the Premier Inn, it was fine. But like my previous night in a proper bed, I tossed and turned all night, not really getting a very good sleep.

CHAPTER 12
Homewards

*"Roll a number, write another song
Like Jimmy heard the day he caught the train"*

- Ocean Colour Scene

I woke to my alarm after another restless night, very aware that today I didn't need to walk very far at all. There wasn't a lot of point in hanging around in a room with nothing more than a bed and a sink, so I got down off the bed carefully, washed my face and cleaned my teeth. Without much to pack up I got into my clothes for the day - my already familiar standard "smart" attire of running leggings, waterproof trousers and my long-sleeved black merino top.

Last time Eva booked the hostel for me she ordered me a breakfast bap for the next morning, but with a better setup kitchen here she chose the option of a full English. I went along for my booked breakfast time of 8am, assuming it was in the same room as I sat last night with my beer which turned out to be correct - a rare navigation success! It was a decent breakfast too, which I enjoyed and cleaned the plate.

I judged that the train station was maybe a 20-minute walk away, and I had a little under 2 hours before the train went. I had nothing else to do here, so I decided that I might as well leisurely wander down and watch some trains while drinking coffee. For a change, I was looking forward to being able to look around and take in my surroundings rather than charge past at a rate of knots, the challenge for the day being some distant destination.

The first part of the walk from the hostel was on a back road lined with big trees, and the moisture in the air combined with the bright early morning sun created stunning sunbeams and such an atmospheric scene. I tried to capture some of the beauty with my phone camera as I wasn't in any sort of rush, but it was a bit difficult to get a photo with my phone of anything that really felt like it represented what I saw, so the reality exists more as a beautiful view in my memory.

The station was in the same direction as the pub I came from yesterday, so I knew the route and it was mostly downhill. For the first morning in over a week, there was no need to walk quickly. Well, strictly there was no need to walk quickly during the previous week, but I wasn't now involved in a personal daily challenge to get to some far-off point, over some hefty hills in some arbitrary rapid time. I was just dawdling to the station, past the YMCA head office, some accountants and solicitors and a few car parks.

I employed my usual navigation skills to go wrong within 100 yards of the station and end up wandering round a gyratory, then crossed in front of a few busses to the front of the station. The 0945 to Newcastle was outside the station, it's diesel engine chugging away while the train sat stationary. That's a long old journey - 9 hours on the train according to Google (or 152 hours walking the 461 miles with 15,500ft of ascent, in case you're interested). I do like sitting on a train looking out the window, but 9 hours on the same one is a bit much - I was glad my trip was only 5 hours and had a mid-way change.

I bought a very nice coffee and a chocolate croissant from the mobile catering van outside the station entrance and sat down, watching people go about their daily business. I spent some time staring out between buildings and trees to the bits I could see of the distant hills where I'd either come from, or should have been going on to, had I not finished my walk now.

I had some time to kill after my coffee and croissant, so I walked back up to the shopping street via a pedestrian crossing with the longest wait time in the UK (not officially confirmed, but it took a bloody long time to change!). The ubiquitous Tesco Express shouted out from its spot up the hill, and I got myself a couple of bottles of sparkling water. Old habits die hard, it felt wrong not having a bottle in each of the pockets on the side of my pack. I also didn't want to pay train prices for water.

Even though it's the furthest station west and a terminus, Penzance station isn't particularly big. Trains were going every half an hour or so from one of the 4 platforms, and my train was sitting waiting quite a long time before its scheduled 10:15am departure. I'd booked my ticket on an app and it had automatically allocated me a seat in coach J. Entering the platform, I saw the first coach was A. It looked like I was going to be walking more than I thought today.

This is a book about my walking on the South West Coast Path, so I'll leave the details of my train journey home out. The surprising facts are that the train left on time (first surprise), arrived at Exeter on time (second surprise), and the second train arrived on time (third surprise). It also kept to time for about three quarters of the rest of the journey, before returning to a characteristically British 10 minutes late by Salisbury.

CHAPTER 13
Epilogue

"Some things cannot be taught; they must be experienced. You never learn the most valuable lessons in life until you go through your own journey."

- Roy T. Bennett

I started writing something about how I felt looking back at my adventure in a previous chapter, but decided I'd wait until the end to put some proper thoughts together. As I write this, it's a few weeks on from my return and I've still not fully processed it.

I planned to walk 630 miles in 21 days… and didn't. So, was it a failure?

No. I don't think it was.

Let's get a few negatives out the way first, a few lessons. My inexperience with the bit that wasn't about moving each day (i.e., sleeping mainly, but also planning and getting food) showed. And my mental state when I got really tired through lack of sleep bit me hard, but I sort-of knew that was likely to happen and had at least some plan in place before I started, which was to not *actually* quit if I felt low, but have a few days to think about it. As I've mentioned before, I think maybe if I'd done some multi-day practice events where I was fully self-sufficient, at least to the point of having to find somewhere to buy food and camp, I may have managed to meet and at least be aware of some of the potential issues. But there's also the chance I may have had such a negative experience that I didn't even try to do the whole SWCP.

But there were a bunch of things on the positive side. Having done almost exclusively single days of training, and only one long day of 30 miles, I did wonder how I was going to physically cope with multiple days hiking over 30 miles. But when put to the test, that wasn't an issue at all. At most I felt a little worn out after the long days. I had no leg pains, no hip pains, no back pains, no shin splints, no foot or ankle problems. Day after day, I felt like walking was no issue as long as I had enough energy from food and wasn't too tired.

I've read about a lot of other people who have all sorts of issues with back, hips, legs and feet. I can only assume the fact that I've been running 40-50 miles per week for quite a few years must have prepared my legs and body a good amount for the walk. Walking has a lower impact than running as you always have one foot on the ground taking some weight, but I was carrying a heavy pack and also walking for a lot more hours continuously than I was used to running. And in my training, I'd covered several hundred miles walking with the pack on, a lot of that time I was covering miles unnecessarily fast in 14 or 15 minutes in order to stress my body to adapt.

Apart from the first few days, the camping really seemed to come together too. By the last night at the Land's End YHA, I was as happy with camping as if I had been in a bed. Setting the tent up was easy and quick, I had routines for setting up and tearing down, and I even found settling down on that mattress in (or under) the sleeping bag really comfortable. Add in the atmosphere in the tent - the vague light, the sounds of nature like wind, trees rustling, animals, birds etc - and once you get used to it, it's not just a nice place, but the best place! I am mindful of the fact I didn't really have to suffer rain or wind though, and I think if I'd had to set up in a storm or spend all night lying awake wondering if the tent would blow away, I may be writing a very different paragraph here.

Overall, I was really lucky with the weather. In the early days, the mornings were misty, shielding me from the sun so I didn't bake. Only on the third day did the sun become a problem, starting to hit from Bideford, getting irritating by Northam Burrows and then baking from Westward Ho! to Clovelly. But the other days were cool and grey in the mornings, with nothing more than hints of rain really, and generally clear and bright in the afternoons.

It's worth clarifying my thoughts on sleep (or lack of it) too. I mentioned in a previous chapter that you can function perfectly well on less sleep, or far more disrupted sleep, than you think. But I also think that this comes with a caveat: it depends how much *thinking* you do during the day. Studies on athletes have shown that physical performance isn't really affected by lack of sleep, but we can all attest to the fact that your brain can end up quite muddled if you have one or more rubbish nights.

My day job involves thinking a lot: architecting complex software systems, managing a company and all sorts of other brain-heavy tasks. Physically, I sit on my butt in a chair – or occasionally raise my desk up to standing position, remember it's hard work standing up all day and go back to sitting for another 3 weeks. But my brain gets a daily bashing, and some days I go home exhausted even though I've hardly got out the seat.

If I have a late night, my thinking goes down the pan and it can get very frustrating. But switch from a low-physical-high-mental task like my work, to a high-physical-low-mental task like walking the coast path, and I think I am in a much, much better place to deal with lack of sleep. A tired brain can make the physical work seem harder, but in a beautiful place like most of the coast path, the distraction of the views and the terrain counterbalance this and I felt I could survive – thrive even – on significantly less sleep than in "normal life".

I've got more of an understanding of the areas I prefer on the coast path. I'm deliberately not using the words *like* and *dislike* or

211

love and *hate*, because I have this stupid, irrational bond with the whole path to the point where even if I'm not particularly enjoying an area, I'm still very happy to be there as it's part of that mesmerising, captivating path, each point has a connection with all those other places I really love.

On the flip side… I'm not generally the biggest fan of the big seaside towns. I think maybe having grown up in Poole and Bournemouth, I have memories of boring shopping trips, rainy days, and crowded areas. Having been exposed to so much of the beach or marine coastal town areas when younger, it loses some of its magic. So, for me, places like Ilfracombe, Woolacombe and Newquay, as well as the river estuary sections from Braunton to Barnstaple and Bideford, were less enjoyable. But stick me on a hilly dirt path cut in a cliff next to the sea or surrounded by mines and engine houses and I don't care what gradient you throw at me, how much mud there is or whether it's raining or windy - I *love* it! The weather and mud won't stop me swearing a lot, but there's still very few places I'd rather be.

Should I have stopped early? That one's more difficult to answer, and was the result of a cascading set of events. First, the exhaustion on day 3. Then once I'd missed a section, it was impossible to finish what I'd set out to do, which took a lot of the meaning from the challenge. Once that had happened, it was much easier to justify dropping more, like Padstow to Newquay, and by that point it felt like I was just out for a hike, like the whole point of the challenge was now lost. And that made it easy

212

to pick a finishing point a few days later, once I'd had the chance to walk over a few bits I knew I loved.

So maybe in hindsight, the biggest lesson learnt from this is two-fold. First, you *will* get tired… you will get *exhausted*, and you *will* want to quit. By all means, take a day off, take it easy, extend your time on the path, but DON'T skip a chunk to do it. Otherwise, soon after, the point of the whole exercise disappears.

I don't really know how to finish this, so I thought I'd just write a few notes to myself that might be useful if I were ever to try this again:

Best bit of kit?

I think I'd have to say my poles. I used them for 90% of the time, and there's nothing quite like half-skiing down a hill on loose gravel with poles, or catching a fall for the 8th time in a single morning!

Oh, and those chocolate-covered coffee beans!

Worst part of the whole adventure?

The despair I felt not being able to find anywhere to camp outside of Braunton. Having said that, although I remember just how overwhelmed I felt at that point… I actually look back on it now quite fondly as, strangely, it was… *exciting* too.

Best part of the whole adventure?

That has to be my favourite bit of the whole coast path (at least of the bits I've visited): Geevor mine near Pendeen down to a little north of Sennen Cove. Amazing landscape, fantastic views, lots of mines and engine houses, caves in the rocks, boulders to climb over, hills, beaches, heather and the sea, and one of my favourite places in the world, Cape Cornwall.

Biggest lesson learnt?

Take an easy day if you need it – in fact, when planning, try and add a flexible buffer that you can take when you need it.

But **do not** skip a section. If your plan is to walk the whole path, do NOT miss any of it out, even if you don't get to the end. As soon as you miss a bit it breaks the whole endeavour.

Also, don't underestimate the effect that disappearing for a few weeks will have on those still at home. It can be all too easy to get caught up in the planning and excitement of *your* adventure, but make sure you give due consideration to those left behind.

Are you going to have another go?

Abso-bloody-lutely! Just don't tell my wife!

TO BE CONTINUED…

THE END

Before you go…

I genuinely hope you've enjoyed this book. If you did and have a few minutes to spare, I would be so grateful if you could leave a review (hopefully positive!) on Amazon, and maybe rave about how amazing it was to spend a few hours getting lost in these pages to all your friends on social media!

You can stay in touch over at:

www.swcpplod.co.uk

and if you've got any questions or feedback, you can use the contact form or social media links on the site.

Thanks again for taking the time to read my book!